THE
ORDNANCE SURVEY
GREAT BRITISH
TREASURE HUNT

Can you solve over 350
clues on a puzzle adventure
from your own home?

Ordnance
Survey

By Ordnance Survey
and Tim Dedopulos

TRAPEZE

Mapping images © Crown Copyright and database rights 2020
Photograph p179 © Julyan Bayes
All other images © Shutterstock
Text and puzzles © The Orion Publishing Group Ltd 2020
Puzzles by Tim Dedopulos

The right of the Ordnance Survey Limited to be identified as
the authors of this work has been asserted in accordance with the
Copyright, Designs and Patents Act 1988.

This edition first published in Great Britain in 2020 by
Trapeze
an imprint of the Orion Publishing Group Ltd
Carmelite House
50 Victoria Embankment
London EC4Y 0DZ

An Hachette UK Company

1 3 5 7 9 10 8 6 4 2

A CIP catalogue record for this book is available from the British Library.

ISBN (Trade Paperback) 978 1 4091 9511 5
ISBN (eBook) 978 1 4091 9512 2

Printed in Italy

The names OS and Ordnance Survey and the OS logos are protected by UK trade
mark registrations and/or are trademarks of Ordnance Survey Limited, Great Britain's
national mapping agency.

Every effort has been made to fulfil requirements with regard to
reproducing copyright material. The author and publisher will be
glad to rectify any omissions at the earliest opportunity.

www.orionbooks.co.uk

MIX
Paper from
responsible sources
FSC® C023419

CONTENTS

PUZZLES

FOREWORD

The sound of treading on tightly packed snow is very distinctive, somewhere between a squeak and a crunch… almost a pop underfoot. That's the sound that always reminds me of the micro-adventures my dad Michael would take me on from Sheffield, where we lived when I was growing up. Sometimes in mid-winter we'd head to Hathersage in the Hope Valley, about 11 miles away. We'd go in that direction because the snow in winter was so deep: great big curvaceous bluey-white drifts taller than him (he's six foot four) that seemed gigantic to me.

In the boot of his Rover he'd always pack a flask of something hot and a spade. And then we would dig. And dig. And dig. Long, intricate connecting tunnels, and he would shape me bricks out of the dense snow, so that I could build walls for our snow caves. I was a princess in her snow castle long before Elsa in *Frozen*. And then when we got home, we'd draw a map of our abandoned settlement, marking the coordinates so we could identify where we'd left the rocks in the snow when we returned, but, of course, Arendelle had melted by then.

Outdoor adventures with children are so important and I realise now how much patience my Dad had. The snow tunnels, the hikes across the Peak District, teaching me to track and tickle trout in rivers near Buxton. I don't think I've matched him yet, but my kids play with a lot of sticks; we have treasure hunts in the garden, and their favourite day last year was a sodden cold October Thursday when I zipped us all up in head-to-toe waterproofs and went out to have a wet leaf fight and roll down some hills.

We all need green spaces (green therapy, I call it) – children and adults alike. It teaches kids independence, builds resilience, immunity, and the free play connected with outdoor exposure (which is basically unstructured playing, so no toys or ready-made entertainment) contributes to their cognitive, physical, social and emotional well-being. Leave a bunch of children outside with nothing but sticks and leaves and watch how they begin to cooperate with each other and use their imagination. For adults, it's key to building our immune system and staying on top of our mental health. The different microbes you breathe in when you're in varying outdoor environments are the good bacteria we need for a healthy microbiome (gut health), which is becoming increasingly recognised as a very important part of our overall health (the microbiome is called the 'second brain' by some medics).

From a psychological point of view, we need nature to ground us and balance our mental health. In the space of a generation many adults have completely lost ALL connections to nature – they don't grow food, touch vegetables before they get packaged up, explore green spaces or touch anything natural in their everyday lives. Nature is permanent. It changes with the seasons, sure, but it is a constant and we humans need that.

However, I have a confession: I have a big sense of adventure but a terrible sense of direction. How swifts manage to return year after year, for sometimes up to twenty years, to the same nest after one of the longest migration journeys in the world (22,000km/14,000 miles) is a mind-boggling miracle to me. I once managed to miss Leeds on the M1. But I do know how to read a map thanks to those early sketches of our snow tunnels, which means I can go out for a hike on my own in those rare moments of solitude – Ordnance Survey map safely tucked in my backpack.

Julia Bradbury, TV Presenter & Co-Founder of The Outdoor Guide

INTRODUCTION

I have been interested in the concept of hunting for buried treasure since reading Kit Williams' *Masquerade* as a boy (look it up, or see Map 27 in this book!). Back then, I dreamed of being the first to solve a series of clues that led to a secret location and getting my hands on a cherished subterranean prize. Of course, nowadays, it wouldn't be right for me to advocate trespassing on a farmer's field or digging a series of unwanted holes in communal parkland, but there are plenty of other ways to experience Britain's hidden delights – this book being one of them!

It is clear that 2020 has been a challenge for all of us, and it has not been the year for travelling around Britain on a treasure hunt, or for exploring our island's beautiful and diverse landscapes. That lifelong dream of walking the entire length of one of our spectacular National Trails may have to wait for another year, but will hopefully soon be achievable. At the time of writing this, many of you will have been spending more time indoors than normal, keeping safe, keeping yourself and others entertained, perhaps with a puzzle book in hand.

At Ordnance Survey, staying in isn't in our genes, but this year we have had to change our messaging and keep people appropriately informed. Our purpose is to help more people to get outside more often, and our GetOutside initiative is designed to motivate people to discover the best Britain has to offer. It sits at the heart of everything we do. Throughout the changing scenarios, we have been using this platform to help people get outside safely, in line with the latest advice from government, local authorities and other organisations.

We're not used to being told where we can and can't go, and we're not used to restrictions on the amount of time we spend outside. In 2020, this outdoor leisure time has become a luxury, a privilege. We have been asked to think long and hard about how we spend these moments outside with our families and loved ones. It is likely that the events of this year will lead to long term behavioural change for many of us. Visits to our multi-award-winning OS Maps app have increased dramatically, as users have looked for new walking routes from their doorsteps. Bicycle sales have boomed.

Lockdown restrictions are being eased, but we can't be sure what the future holds. Some of the locations referred to in this book may not fully be open for business yet, or are operating in new and unfamiliar conditions. As ever, it is hard to do Britain justice in only 40 maps, but we've done our best to bring together a variety of interesting and inspiring settings. This book will not ask you to dig any literal holes, but it will encourage you to study maps in different ways, identifying features and searching for clues that at first seem elusive. *The Ordnance Survey Great British Treasure Hunt* is intended as a celebration of travelling around Britain with eyes wide open and an adventurous spirit: asking questions, looking for something new.

I like to think we all have hidden treasures in Britain, a place or view that may not be widely known to the masses, but is close to our hearts. For many of us in 2020 this is likely to have been closer to home, and made even more special. We'd love to hear your suggestions on our social media pages, using the tag #OSTreasureHunt. Find us on Twitter @OSleisure, Instagram @ordnancesurvey and Facebook @osmapping.

For the latest information, guidance and inspiration, please visit **getoutside.uk**. I look forward to seeing you all outside more often in 2021!

Nick Giles, Managing Director – Ordnance Survey Leisure

COMMON MAP ABBREVIATIONS AND SYMBOLS

SELECTED TOURIST AND LEISURE SYMBOLS

	Art gallery (notable / important)		Museum
	Boat hire		National Trust
	Boat trips		Nature reserve
	Building of historic interest		Other tourist feature
	Cadw (Welsh Heritage)		Parking
	Camp site		Park and ride, all year
	Camping and caravan site		Park and ride, seasonal
	Caravan site		Phone; public, emergency
	Castle or fort		Picnic site
	Cathedral or abbey		Preserved railway
	Country park		Public house(s)
	Craft centre		Public toilets
	Cycle hire		Recreation, leisure or sports centre
	Cycle trail		Slipway
	English Heritage		Theme or pleasure park
	Fishing		Viewpoint
	Garden or arboretum		Visitor centre
	Golf course or links		Walks or trails
	Heritage centre		Water activities (board)
	Historic Scotland		Water activities (paddle)
	Horse riding		Water activities (powered)
	Information centre		Water activities (sailing)
	Information centre, seasonal		Watersports centre (multi-activity)
	Mountain bike trail		World Heritage site / area

ABBREVIATIONS

Acad	Academy	Ind Est	Industrial Estate	Rd	Road
BP	Boundary Post	La	Lane	Rems	Remains
BS	Boundary Stone	LC	Level Crossing	Resr	Reservoir
CG	Cattle Grid	Liby	Library	Rly	Railway
CH	Clubhouse	Mkt	Market	Sch	School
Cotts	Cottages	Meml	Memorial	St	Saint / Street
Dis	Disused	MP	Milepost	Twr	Tower
Dismtd	Dismantled	MS	Milestone	TH	Town Hall
Fm	Farm	Mon	Monument	Uni	University
F Sta	Fire Station	PH	Public House	NTL	Normal Tidal Limit
FB	Footbridge	P, PO	Post Office	Wks	Works
Ho	House	Pol Sta	Police station	°W; Spr	Well; Spring

PUBLIC RIGHTS OF WAY

- - - - - - - - - - -	Footpath	**The representation on the maps of any**
— — — — —	Bridleway	**other road, track or path is no evidence**
+—+—+—+—+	Byway open to all traffic	**of the existence of a right of way.**
⊥—⊤—⊥—⊤—⊥	Restricted byway (not for use by mechanically propelled vehicles)	

The symbols show the defined route so far as the scale of mapping will allow. Rights of way are liable to change and may not be clearly defined on the ground. Please check with the relevant local authority for the latest information. Rights of way are not shown on maps of Scotland, where rights of responsible access apply.

PUBLIC ACCESS

• • •   Other routes with public access (not normally shown in urban areas)

◆ ◆ ◆   National Trail 🚶, Scotland's Great Trails (🏃),
European Long Distance Route and selected recreational routes

ACCESS LAND (England and Wales)

Access land

Access land in wooded area

within sand

Coastal margin

Access land portrayed on this map is intended as a guide to land normally available for access on foot, for example access land created under the Countryside and Rights of Way Act 2000, and land managed by National Trust, Forestry England, Woodland Trust and Natural Resources Wales. Some restrictions will apply; some land shown as access land may not have open access rights; always refer to local signage.

The depiction of rights of access does not imply or express any warranty as to its accuracy or completeness. Observe local signs and follow the Countryside Code. Visit: **gov.uk/government/publications/the-countryside-code**

OTHER ACCESS (Scotland)

National Trust for Scotland, always open

National Trust for Scotland, limited access – observe local signs

Forestry and Land Scotland, normally open – observe local signs

Woodland Trust Land

All land within the 'coastal margin' (where it already exists) is associated with the England Coast Path (**nationaltrail.co.uk/england-coast-path**) and is by default access land, but in some areas it contains land not subject to access rights – for example cropped land, buildings and their curtilage, gardens and land subject to local restrictions including many areas of saltmarsh and flats that are not suitable for public access. The coastal margin is often steep, unstable and not readily accessible. Please take careful note of conditions and local signage on the ground.

In Scotland, everyone has access rights in law* over most land and inland water, provided access is exercised responsibly. The **Scottish Outdoor Access Code** is the reference point for responsible behaviour, and can be obtained at **outdooraccess-scotland.com**.

LAND FEATURES

⁞⁞⁞⁞⁞	Cutting, embankment	⅄ Beacon 𝕀 Mast		Gravel pit	
⬤►	Bus or coach station	Lighthouse		Sand pit	
■	Bunkhouse camping barn, or other hostel	Lighthouse; disused		Other pit or quarry	
△	Triangulation pillar	𝕀 Wind pump		Landfill site or slag/spoil heap	
+	Place of worship	丫 Wind turbine			
	Current or former place of worship;	𝕏 Windmill (with or without sails)	Building; important building		
▮	with tower				
●	with spire, minaret or dome	🕎 Solar Farm	Glasshouse or structure		

THE ORDNANCE SURVEY GREAT BRITISH TREASURE HUNT

AN INTRODUCTION TO THE PUZZLES

You are about to embark on a puzzle adventure around Great Britain. It's a journey as eccentric as your guide, the redoubtable Aunt Bea, snaking its way across the land, taking in a wide range of fascinating sites. No adventure of this sort could ever be definitive and there were stops that could not be made and will have to wait for next time. We hope that, like Aunt Bea, you will be inspired to explore the rich treasures to be found all around us.

The puzzles she has uncovered contain something for everyone: a mix of word puzzles, search-and-find clues and general knowledge questions, as well as navigation conundrums to satisfy the more skilled map-readers.* Pay careful attention to Aunt Bea in the sections before the puzzles too, as she's been known to give away clues. You may sometimes even have to find answers to questions that can't be solved with the maps, so keep your wits about you.

Questions are split into four levels of difficulty:

- **Easy**
- **Medium**
- **Tricky**
- **Challenging**

Once you have completed all 40 sets of puzzles, you'd be forgiven for thinking you've conquered the book, but there is still one challenge to overcome. Each map has a Key Puzzle, which, once solved, can be used to work out the final location of the treasure on page 187.

We hope you finish this adventure celebrating the hidden treasures to be found all around us and that these maps, stories and puzzles encourage you to think again about your local area, to perhaps take a look at a map and imagine, as Aunt Bea does, those that have walked upon it and in whose footprints you can follow.

* For those of you that aren't map whizzes just yet, remember the following:
ground survey heights are marked on the maps as black numbers, air survey heights are marked as orange numbers, and the vertical interval between contour lines is usually 5 metres but in mountainous regions it may well be 10 metres, so be careful!

LETTER FROM AUNT BEA

Have you ever been really bored of staying in your house? I *definitely* was before my aunt, Bea, decided to take me on an adventure.

You need to know a bit about Aunt Bea. She's actually my mother's aunt, but I only ever tried to call her great-aunt once, and her ferocious scowl was all the hint I needed. It's hard to work out how old she is, but my guess is somewhere between 50 and 75. Probably. She has silvery hair and glasses and an accent that can't seem to decide quite where it's from. We won't hear from her for months at a time, then she'll appear suddenly at the door with a battered leather bag and a whole load of new stories.

I've always been a bit unclear about what she did before she retired. It involved something to do with paintings or furniture, and travelling the world. A running joke in the family was that she'd been a spy, but whenever I asked her, she'd just narrow her eyes and say, 'What kind of spy would I be if I told *you*?'

One thing I do know is that she's always been obsessed with seeing as much of the country as possible. She claims our ancestor was part of the original Survey of Scotland mapping party with William Roy in 1747, the one that the Ordnance Survey originated with, and insists that exploring is in our blood. I wasn't convinced, not until one rainy Thursday, when a letter arrived.

My dearest nephew,

The family gossip network tells me that you are withering on the vine down there, permanently plugged into some device or other. I fear your brain and legs will have positively atrophied. Fortunately for your constitution, I urgently need you to join me on a trip of vital importance. I've cleared it with the parentals, and I promise you'll find it entertaining.

I've been looking for something for a very long time. A treasure, you might say. A new document has recently come to light, packed with clues and questions. I need your help to solve the problems. In the process, we're going to exercise your legs and your brain, and see if we can't get you a bit more clued up about the island you live on.

(If we're lucky, we may even make our fortunes.)

Please pack a small bag with clothes for a variety of weathers, and join me at your earliest convenience as per the enclosed aeroplane tickets.

Yours excitedly,

Aunt Bea

Two days later, I arrived at Stornoway Airport on the Isle of Lewis in the Outer Hebrides. I was impressed at how clean and modern everything looked. The terminal building was small, but welcoming, and better laid out than the much larger airport I'd departed from. I quickly spotted Aunt Bea, holding up a sign that said 'Soft City Dweller' and smiling wryly.

Once we'd said hello and shared a swift hug, she straightened up. 'There's no time to waste, my boy,' she told me. 'We've got to travel 20 miles west and 5,000 years into the past. Take these.' She handed me a rucksack, and her voice lowered conspiratorially. 'You're going to need them.'

On the way to her car, an ancient dark green thing she called Bertha, I opened the bag. It was full of maps, and jammed among them I spotted a compass and a large, battered, untidy-looking notebook.

As soon as I was seated, I fished out the notebook for a look. I'm not sure what I'd expected, but the book was crammed, cover to cover, with pasted-in clippings and rambling handwritten paragraphs and hasty sketches, interspersed with lists of questions, sets of numbers and all manner of other curiosities. Here and there, Aunt Bea had inserted bits of paper with comments of her own in her distinctive, flowing handwriting.

She glanced over at me, a happy grin on her face. 'Intriguing, isn't it? I know where we start, and I've got some ideas about other steps, but there's observations to be made and questions to be answered. With your help, my boy, I know we'll find the right path.'

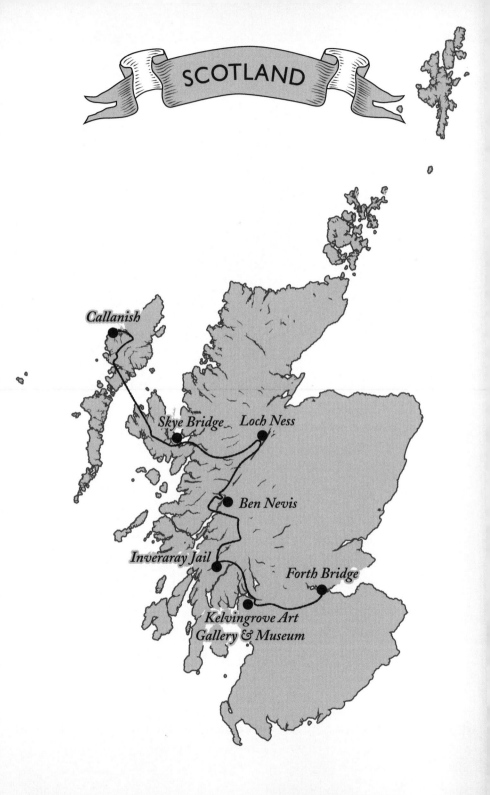

SCOTLAND

Callanish

Skye Bridge   Loch Ness

Ben Nevis

Inveraray Jail

Forth Bridge

Kelvingrove Art
Gallery & Museum

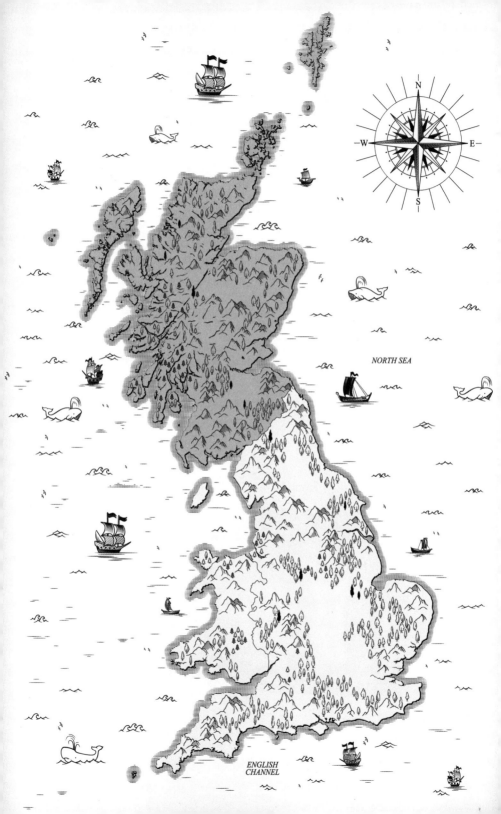

NORTH SEA

ENGLISH
CHANNEL

Map 1 CALLANISH

We drove through a landscape rolling with grassy plains and small, glittering lochs and Aunt Bea kept up a steady monologue.

'People are obsessed with John O'Groats and that's fine, but you can give me Callanish any day. If you travel east from John O'Groats you get to Norway which is very interesting and all. But if you travel west from the Callanish Stones, over the hills and lochs, you scrape by Greenland and carry on to Newfoundland! We're right on the edge of Europe here, with nothing much at all to shield us from the North Atlantic.'

I tried to imagine all that ocean, stretching on to the far side of forever.

'When you first see the circle of stones above Loch Roag, with the hills of Great Bernera in the distance… well, you'll see. It's 2,000 years older than Stonehenge. I can just see those late Neolithic craftspeople, five millennia ago, spending months, years, hauling those great slabs of Lewisian Gneiss—'

My expression must have given me away.

'One of the world's oldest types of rock, dear boy. Up to three billion years old!'

I nodded, impressed.

'Anyway. No one knows why the stones were originally placed there. Some have suggested a prehistoric lunar observatory. We know that people were buried there later from human remains and there has long been speculation that the stones were of some sort of ritualistic importance. Personally, I have always preferred the explanation that the stones were a tribe of giants who were turned to rock when they refused to convert to Christianity.'

She pulled into a car park and stopped, then picked a map from the rucksack. I accepted it, with thanks.

'We have a short but exceptionally beautiful walk ahead of us,' she said. 'And we're going to need this.'

■ Easy

1. What do you get if you subtract the smallest number on the map from the greatest number? = 50

2. How many locations on the map are specifically for livestock management? cattle grid 6

■ Medium

the one neer the road

3. Which cattle grid is the peak of Aird Callanish further from?

4. How many diagonal lines touch the north-east side of the A858 along the stretch of road between the school and the public telephone? 21

■ Tricky

5. Callanish, on the Isle of Lewis, is within which archipelago? *outer he-rio -s*

6. Counting from the top, which full or partial grid row of the map contains the most wells, and how many is that?

■ Challenging

7. From the westerly pier, head directly south to a yellow road. Follow that to a jetty, and then move directly east to the third different contour line you meet. Trace that line to a school, and from the school, move west to a complete island. What is it called?

8. Can you discover the number of monoliths in the celebrated stone circle of the Callanish Stones? Solving this anagram will be useful to you: A BRONZE DESK.

○ Key Puzzle

* The word 'Eilean' appears in black more than once on this map. What does it mean?

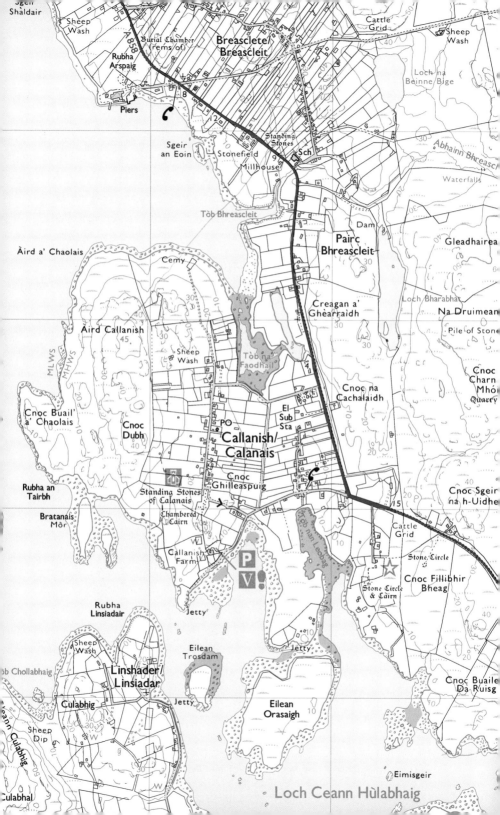

Map 2 SKYE BRIDGE

From what we learned at Callanish, it was clear that our next destination was to be the Lochalsh peninsula, and, specifically, the bridge from the Scottish mainland to the Isle of Skye. I found it odd that we were going from a place so ancient to one that was opened in 1995.

'Aunt Bea, don't get me wrong, those standing stones were amazing but I'm just not sure we're going to find many of your ancient clues at a bridge that's only in its twenties.'

'It's an interesting *contrast*, I'll give you that,' Aunt Bea said. 'But don't underestimate bridges, even recent ones. When you're crossing a bridge, you're always *between*, in a place of transition. Liminal, like twilight, neither here nor there. Good word, liminal. What better spot to be to unravel a puzzle that moves you from place to place?'

I agreed that it did seem appropriate.

'This bridge brings us from the Hebrides to Ross, from archipelago to the mainland of Great Britain, and it does so in style, via Eilean Bàn, the White Island. Skye is ancient, steeped in perhaps 10,000 years of history. And keep an eye out – if you see something that looks like a big tomcat's head in the water, it's an otter. The village on the mainland side, Kyle of Lochalsh, is also pleasingly resonant – it's almost exactly 500 miles north of Land's End. Everything fits together, you see, like a cunningly tied knot.'

We stopped off in a place marked on the map as Kyleakin, a picturesque village that apparently takes its name from King Haakon the Old of Norway, and we strolled along the water's edge.

'This was where the original ferry used to cross to the mainland in the seventeenth century. The ferryman is of course a key figure in both Greek and Roman mythology. He who carries us from the land of the living across the rivers of the dead. An island nation surrounded by more than 6,000 islands. We are a nation of ferrymen, never forget that. I sometimes think it informs our national character, to be
so permanently reminded. Now, cheese and pickle or egg and cress?'

As we ate, we pulled out the right map, and, brushing crumbs away, compared notes and questions and map information with the views in front of us, and thought about where we were to go next.

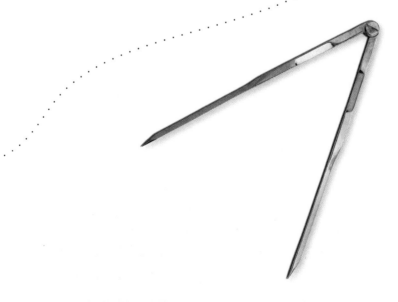

▨ Easy

1. Symbols for which tourist and leisure facilities appear on the Plock of Kyle, north of the A-road and west of the train tracks?

2. Is the Post Office closer to Kyle House or to Coolin View?

▨ Medium

3. How many schools are shown on the Isle of Skye (south-west of map)?

4. According to the famous traditional song, who was carried over the sea to Skye?

▨ Tricky

5. The Isle of Skye is part of which archipelago?

6. Which is taller, the highest peak shown on Skye or the highest peak shown on the mainland, and by how much?

▨ Challenging

7. Can you piece together the following fragments to make four words that appear on the map? AID, AL, CAI, DR, GAR, LLI, NM, NNE, OCH, ORE, SGI, STE

8. Subtract the total number of hotels on the map from the value of a number printed in black on the Isle of Skye. Divide the result by the sum of the number of times 'Cnoc' and 'Kyle' are printed on the map in black ink to get a whole number. Compare this to the number of National Trust for Scotland locations shown on the map. What is the difference?

🔍 Key Puzzle

* The name of a loch is printed directly south of a hill whose name means 'Hill of the Loch'. What is it?

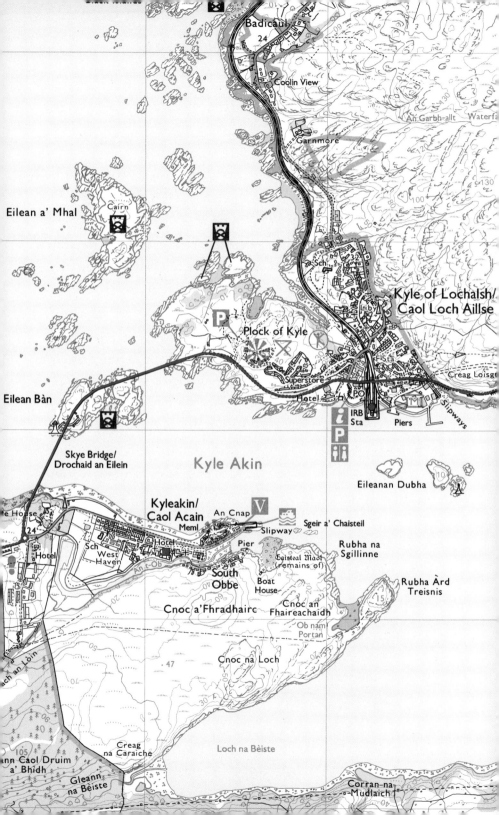

Map 3 LOCH NESS

The drive from the bridge to Loch Ness was incredible – a single road that wound its way past hills and lochs, stone and grass, the dark edges of long straight-trunked pinewood forests and the yellow of gorse flowers.

After about two hours of Aunt Bea declaring the names of everything we passed – 'Loch Alsh, Loch Duich, Sgurr Fhuaran…' – we arrived at the edge of the loch.

Aunt Bea told me we were only 25 miles from Inverness, the capital of the Highlands, a bustling city and the location of King Duncan's murder by Macbeth in Shakespeare's play; ironically it's also the happiest place in Scotland, according to recent surveys.

You'd never know it, though. The loch is huge and dark, and it feels like a place that keeps hold of secrets. The water is full of peat, so even right at the shoreline it's almost impossible to see much through it. Even on a sunny day, there's a sense of majesty to the loch, a feeling that it has little interest in human affairs. Like we're beneath its regard.

The loch is best known for the legend of the monster, of course. The idea that there's a gigantic sea-serpent hiding in those black waters seems a lot

less silly when you're actually there. But in a way, the creature feels like an attempt to make the loch friendlier, less forbidding. Easier to deal with. That's how I felt, anyway.

'If it's just a story, it's one we've been telling ourselves for a long time, my boy,' said Aunt Bea, as we set out around the east edge of the lake. 'There are reports of a man being dragged under by a water beast as early as the sixth century. And there have been around a thousand sightings since then. There have been all sorts of theories – a plesiosaur, a lost Greenland shark, a giant sturgeon or even an enormous eel. The way I see it, what better place to hide treasure than with a monster to guard it.'

We stood at the shore and watched the small waves lift in the breeze.

'It's about 126 fathoms deep, more than 750 feet – you could sink St Paul's Cathedral in there and never see the dome.'

I tried not to imagine that black water stretching down and ever down from my feet.

I shook the image out of my head. We had puzzles to solve.

Easy

1. What is the smallest named lake on the map?

2. Are there more Carns or Creags shown on the map?

Medium

3. To the nearest 25m, what is the elevation of the picnic site?

4. Loch Ness is the first among the lakes of the British Isles in which physical regard?

Tricky

5. If we estimate Loch Ness to be exactly 56 square kilometres in surface area, what volume would its monstrous inhabitant have to be in order to raise the water level by one eight-hundredth of a millimetre when fully submerged?

6. What's the difference between the highest and lowest elevations marked on the map?

Challenging

7. What do the words 'am', 'hi', 'nigh' and 'it' have in common?

8. Can you discover which notorious English mountaineer, poet and ritualist owned a house shown on the map? Keep in mind you'll have to CORRELATE WISELY.

Key Puzzle

* Take the ground survey height near the name of the one glen shown on the map – it's in the north-east quadrant – and multiply it by 10. Then, to the result, add the number of named creags shown. What's the total?

Map 4 BEN NEVIS

'So, from 750 feet deep to 4,400 feet high,' said Aunt Bea, as we approached the foothills of Ben Nevis. 'Not a bad differential at all.' We pulled into a car park and got out to stretch our legs.

'I'm sure you'll excuse me if I don't drag you up to the summit,' Aunt Bea began, rubbing the small of her back. 'My knees are not exactly what they used to be, and I'm not entirely convinced that your dear parents would be sympathetic, were anything unfortunate to happen to you.'

Looking up at the peaks disappearing into cloud and mist, I didn't complain.

'It used to be a volcano, you know. They think it exploded about a third of a billion years ago, with an explosion large enough to shake the ground thousands of miles away. Some people translate its name as The Cruel Mountain, others as Cloud-Top Mountain or The Mountain of Heaven, but no one is actually sure. It's quite the presence either way, eh?'

I nodded.

'The pony trail up to the summit is reasonably safe as these things go, but we really would need the right boots and clothing for any amount of serious hiking. Bertha has acquired all sorts of equipment over the years, but walking up there is still not something to take lightly.'

She gazed up at the peak.

'Keats climbed it when he was 23 years old, you know, only a couple of years before he died of tuberculosis.' Aunt Bea spread her feet out wider and held her hand out to the mountain. 'Mist is spread / Before the earth, beneath me – even such, / Even so vague is man's sight of himself!'

I checked around to see if there was anyone watching us and I thought
of all the people who had climbed the mountain, long before the age of
waterproofs and specialist equipment. I thought of those people who had
dragged those massive stones to Callanish all those
thousands of years ago. Had they even known that
this place existed? Before maps, when 200 miles
away was a different world.

'A few of us got as high as the abandoned
meteorological station one year during the summer
break, but we never reached the summit.'

Part of me wondered if she was going to change her
mind and make an ascent that afternoon but then
she shook her head.

'Anyway,' said Aunt Bea, 'we'll walk for about half
an hour and then check the clues. There's plenty to
be getting on with from down here.'

Easy

1. Ben Nevis is the highest peak of where?
2. How many times does the word 'Cairn' appear in English on the map?

Medium

3. What is the smallest number printed in orange on the map?
4. Which is higher up: a) the castle, b) the observatory, c) the cave?

Tricky

5. The Càrn Mòr Dearg Arête links Ben Nevis and Càrn Mòr Dearg. What is an arête?
6. If the columns of the map grid are labelled A to D from left to right, and the rows numbered 1 to 5 from top to bottom, which single grid square contains the greatest vertical disparity?

Challenging

7. From the number of the lowest ground survey height on the map, head eastwards to a coniferous tree, and then north to a letter which is also touched by a contour line. Head directly north from there until you pass through another word printed in black ink. What tall structure is nearby?
8. Can you discover the name of the scientist whose observations while on Ben Nevis eventually led to him earning a Nobel Prize? He's present in HETEROCHRONISM SALLOWNESS.

Key Puzzle

* Leaving the car park, note the first ground survey height you come to. Take the first two digits of that number and reverse them, then add this to the original number, and when you have a total, halve it. What is the result?

Map 5 INVERARAY JAIL

'The plot thickens. Do not pass go, do not collect £200,' muttered Aunt Bea, her eyes twinkling, as we'd headed back towards Bertha at Ben Nevis. As we travelled south, down through those steep hills and past dark-watered lochs, she began talking wistfully.

'When Caesar first conquered this island, it was such a wild place: huge expanses of forest, reaching to the mountains, impenetrable marshes. And the animals! Wild boar, elk, beavers, bears, bison, the horned urus and wolves. Even when we cut down the forests for farmland, drained the marshes, the mighty wolf endured still.'

As we passed by the shores of Loch Linnhe, she pointed to an island just visible through the mist.

'Do you know the tradition of burying bodies on the islands in lochs is thought to be so the wolves wouldn't get them. There are accounts of wolves beyond the mid-1700s in these parts.'

We sat in silence, both of us lost in thoughts of the wild past.

Arriving into Inveraray felt like entering a different era. It was a neat collection of pretty buildings at the western shore of Loch Fyne.

As Aunt Bea explained it, the whole town was completely redesigned and rebuilt during the late 1700s, mostly by a talented architect from Edinburgh named Robert Mylne. Part of the reason that the town was rebuilt was to move it further away from Inveraray Castle, where the fifth Duke of Argyll and head of the Campbell clan lived and his descendants still do. It looks out over the River Aray, perfect, like a child's toy castle. We wandered through the picturesque streets and then stood by the side of the water. It felt like an exercise in human mastery of the landscape.

Aunt Bea wanted us to see the preserved jailhouse and courthouse they had turned into a museum, as she felt sure a trail of two-hundred-year-old footsteps led there.

'Loch Fyne is the longest of Scotland's sea lochs, famous for the quality of its seafood,' said Aunt Bea, staring into the distance. 'I once knew someone who could eat three dozen oysters in one go you know.' She shook her head, as if clearing her vision. 'Perhaps we'll find somewhere to reward ourselves if we can solve the puzzles soon enough.'

QUESTIONS

▨ Easy

1. What sporting activity is shown as being available on the map?

2. The map shows a pond named after which heavenly body?

▨ Medium

3. If you multiply the number of hotels marked on the map by the number of star-shaped cairns shown, what do you get?

4. Is Inveraray in northern, western, southern or eastern Scotland?

▨ Tricky

5. Which place might be said to be a powerful dwelling?

6. Can you find four different locations on the map whose names include foodstuffs?

▨ Challenging

7. Can you find locations on the map that are anagrams of the following words or phrases? Ignore the spaces and punctuation, which may differ from those in the place names.
   a. BAHRAIN CAT HALL
   b. DISSONANT GENT
   c. BURGH ACHED
   d. CROOKED BYLAW

8. Inveraray Jail is a popular living museum indicated on the map that shows visitors an accurate reconstruction of what life inside would have been like while it was in its original use. Which century does it date from?

🔍 Key Puzzle

* Find a disarranged METRO CAB and, nearby, a location that has taken the same name. What is the rest of that second location's name?

Map 6 KELVINGROVE ART GALLERY AND MUSEUM

'A city has many hearts,' Aunt Bea told me. We were winding our way through Glasgow at the time, heading to our next destination, the Kelvingrove Art Gallery. 'They come in all sorts – social, cultural, financial, mercantile, historical, and on and on. Glasgow has more hearts than most, from the Barrowlands and Sauchiehall Street to Hampden Park and the Armadillo.'

In only just over 60 miles since leaving Inveraray, it felt like we'd entered a different country. A different world. Aunt Bea had pulled the car over in Arden to explain.

'We're pretty much on the Highland Boundary Fault here,' she said. 'It's the geological feature that separates the highlands from the lowlands, a record of continents colliding hundreds of millions of years ago that forced rocks up into mountains. A reminder that underneath the human are always other deeper layers of time, shaping our experiences of what is normal and natural.'

I thought of that as I'd looked out of the window, passing the more familiar human landscapes of houses, cafes and shops, as we entered Glasgow from the west; the land felt suddenly flat as far as the eye could see.

'So many parks,' I said, as we crossed a river and found ourselves alongside another row of trees.

'Some people translate the Gaelic for Glasgow as "our dear green space",' said Aunt Bea.

I looked up at an impressive cathedral.

Aunt Bea noticed my gaze. 'St Mungo's. The oldest building in the city, and the oldest cathedral in Scotland. A perfect

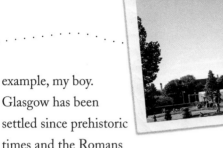

example, my boy. Glasgow has been settled since prehistoric times and the Romans were all around these parts. St Mungo's has been there since the end of the twelfth century, then came the university in the fifteenth century, then the city became a centre for merchants and trade. At the turn of the nineteenth century, it vied to be known as the "Second City of the Empire" with its huge shipyards, its factories and warehouses. Then the two great wars, the Clyde Shipyards closing, the factories, the steelworks going cold. There's never one city, there's hundreds, all built upon the other, different hearts left over from different bodies. Of all of Glasgow's hearts, however, Kelvingrove is my favourite, and I find it deeply encouraging that we're now being led here.

'The park by that name dates back to the 1850s, designed by Joseph Paxton, the same chap who created the Crystal Palace in London. It's a delight, of course. The idea was to preserve some rural loveliness as the city spread, give somewhere for the people to stretch their legs. Like Crystal Palace, the park played host to an international exhibition of art, science and industry in 1888. The Kelvingrove Art Gallery and Museum grew out of that, and it has been a place of wonders and marvels ever since – globally important artworks, one of the world's best collections of weapons and armour, all manner of creatures.

'Just because things are more recent doesn't mean they're any less important. In my eyes, it makes what we've been able to accomplish in so little time all the more remarkable. Keep your wits about you now, my boy, as we explore.'

Easy

1. Which football ground is shown on the map?

2. What is the circular building used as?

Medium

3. Counting from the top, which full or partial grid row of the map contains the most places of worship, and how many is that?

4. In which area is the largest hospital on the map?

Tricky

5. What do the following words have in common?
   Bridge   Inning
   Nock   West

6. From what do Kelvingrove Park and many other surrounding locations take their name?

Challenging

7. Can you discover which controversial masterpiece by Salvador Dalí is housed adjacent to Kelvingrove Park?

8. Starting from the number 11, head south to an academy, and then follow the nearest major road round to the fourth rail station. There's a National Trust for Scotland location nearby. Go directly west, until you intersect an A-road near water. That road is crossed by a B-road. Follow that B-road to a place of worship on a staggered crossroads. What attraction is just to the north?

Key Puzzle

* The Clyde-built, three-masted barque *Glenlee*, constructed in 1896, is shown on the map under its nickname. What is the first word downriver from its location?

Map 7 FORTH BRIDGE

Aunt Bea was not usually silent, but even she found it hard to wax lyrical about the almost 50 miles we had travelled east on the M8, once we'd left the outskirts of Glasgow behind us.

'There's no shame in some roads being about the destination, not the journey,' she said. 'Now dig out the right map for the Forth River.'

North Queensferry is dominated by the Forth Bridge. There's no other word for it. The village is pretty and the people are friendly, but the bridge marches through and over it like a red giant. The locals barely notice it, I suspect, but I found it very difficult to think of anything else – not least because of how it dwarfs everything around it.

'The Firth of Forth is an estuary where several rivers come to the sea, including the River Forth. The word firth shares a common ancestor with the Scandinavian word fjord. There are two other bridges across the Firth of Forth, the Queensferry Crossing that carries the motorway, and the Forth Road Bridge, which is now used for public transport, bicycles and pedestrians. This one, the original and still the best, which carries trains, is significantly more spectacular than the others, 130 years old and going

strong. Ah, those Victorians knew how to do bridges, didn't they! You see how the bridge's support girders rise and fall, like the ridges of a stegosaurus?' Aunt Bea was well aware of my ongoing fondness for dinosaurs.

I nodded.

'Well, each of those pieces is separate, weighted so they balance on their central supports. Cantilevered. Its biggest spans were the longest cantilevered bridge segments in the world for 20 years, until the Quebec Bridge came and stole their thunder, but they're still the second-longest. About 1,700 feet, all in one piece, perfectly engineered and balanced. It's incredible when you think about it. A fitting testament to Scotland's resilience and ingenuity. And a fascinating next step on our path!'

She pointed at a bench that faced out opposite the water and handed me her leather bag full of maps.

'Now, you sit there and puzzle these out and I'll go rustle us up some fish and chips. Something tells me it will soon be time for us to turn our faces south, to those savage lands known as England.'

Easy

1. How many blue marsh symbols are there in St Margaret's Marsh?

2. Which location sounds like it might have been used for executions?

Medium

3. Where on the map might you expect to find a horse?

4. Which of the three bridges is above the Firth of Forth for the greatest distance?

Tricky

5. Which of these names is the odd one out?
   a. Craig   b. Edgar
   c. James   d. Maggie
   e. Piers

6. What is the lowest elevation enumerated on the map?

Challenging

7. Starting at a religious headland, follow the coast southwards to the third marked pier. From there, head straight north to a land-locked ferry. How tall is the nearest hilltop?

8. Which major Fife town is less than ten miles from North Queensferry? Look for a MIRED FUNNEL.

Key Puzzle

* Several words lie between the museum and the blue lady. What is the second you pass through?

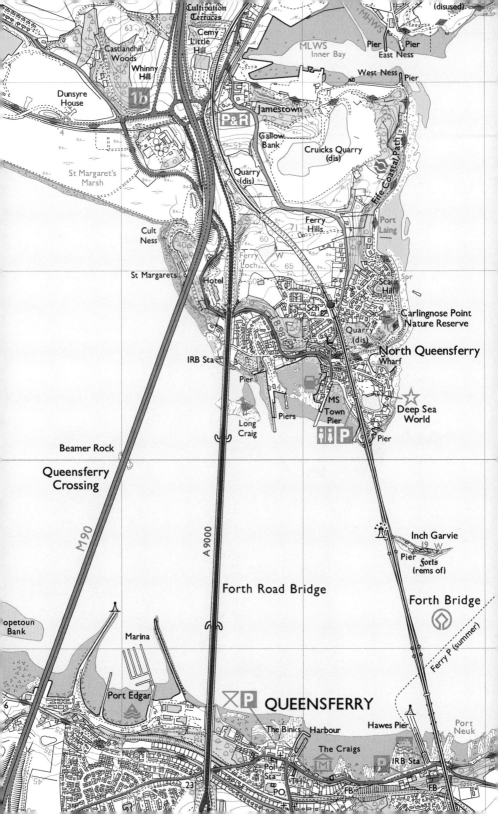

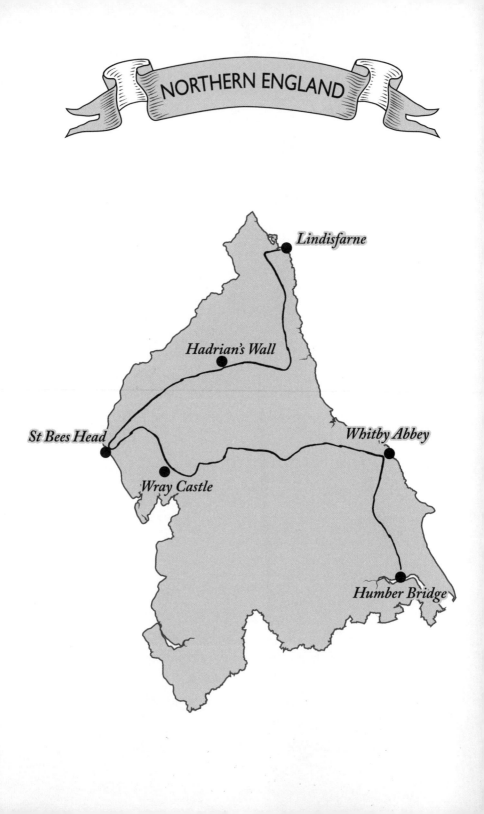

Lindisfarne

Hadrian's Wall

St Bees Head

Wray Castle

Whitby Abbey

Humber Bridge

NORTH SEA

ENGLISH
CHANNEL

Map 8 LINDISFARNE

South of Berwick-upon-Tweed, by about 12 or so miles, the northernmost town in England, the Holy Island of Lindisfarne, is a beautiful but lonely-looking place. In the hours around low tide, you can drive there along the causeway, or walk the ancient Pilgrim's Way, but the rest of the time it's cut off from the mainland. You can certainly see how it was a good place for contemplating the big questions in life.

'There was a priory here by 635 AD,' Aunt Bea told me as we approached. 'It was the cradle of Christianity in the region for centuries. Stories of the violent raid by the Vikings in 793 was the talk of Europe. There were those who couldn't believe that such a holy place could have been allowed to be desecrated by pagans at all. For 300 years, the monks were scattered, only small communities daring to stay in the area. Then the Normans arrived and it was rebuilt in the 1090s. They turned the old structure into a church, St Mary the Virgin, which is still standing, and built a new abbey next to it. Then Henry VIII dissolved all the monasteries in 1536, and the abbey was stripped for stone to help build the castle. Shoddy treatment really for somewhere so significant, but at least the original survives in spirit, if not in stone.' She stood looking across the bay.

'I also always think it's important to remember how what we see isn't how things have always been. That border between Scotland and England feels so much lesser than the border between the highlands and lowlands we crossed in Scotland. Always so important to cross lines on a map in real life. You never really know a place until you do. You can have every map ever made in a device you can fit in your jacket pocket, but until you've actually been there, well, you'll only know it partially.'

Lindisfarne

I looked from the sprawling ruins of the abbey over the bay to the castle, which sat brooding on its small hill.

'There's lots of curious talk about Lindisfarne. Scholars talk of its magnificent illustrated manuscripts and rich religious significance, but wilder sorts like to link it with all manner of legends. Some claim that St Cuthbert still walks the island. My favourite story happened just after Christmas in 877, when Alfred the Great was forced to flee from a surprise attack by the latest Viking leader, a chap called Guthrum, and ended up on the isle of Athelney down in Somerset. For a while, the whole kingdom of England was shrunk down to an island of under 10,000 square metres, but St Cuthbert's ghost spoke to Alfred the Great to reassure the fugitive king that all would be well. Far down in the south-west, in his hour of need, a saint from the far north-east came to his rescue. By Easter the following year he'd counterattacked and starved the Danes into submission and Guthrum converted to Christianity.'

Aunt Bea held out her hand for me to help her up from the bench.

'Maybe if we're lucky enough, we too may get a bit of spiritual guidance here. Some of these puzzles require it I'd say.'

Easy

1. What is the greatest height marked on the map?

2. How many wells are shown on the map?

Medium

3. Lindisfarne lies off which English coast?

4. How many different laws can you find on the map?

Tricky

5. From the most cunning spot on the map, head west to a delicacy, and then north to a sink. Follow the footpath to a black number, and add to it the other black numbers you pass near as you head east to a ruddy bank. What is your total?

6. Is the Emmanuel Head beacon closer to the Water Tower or to Steel End?

Challenging

7. Can you find locations on the map that are anagrams of the following words or phrases? Ignore the spaces and punctuation, which may differ from those in the place names.
   a. PORK LEASEHOLD
   b. LEWD GERBIL
   c. ENDORSING IT
   d. SHINING HEAT

8. A celebrated holy text was created at Lindisfarne, and has been housed in London since the eighteenth century. Can you discover the year in which the island finally received a copy, courtesy of an American scholar? The total 18 will be useful here.

Key Puzzle

* What is the name of the head printed between a 9m and a 12m survey height, one aerial and one ground?

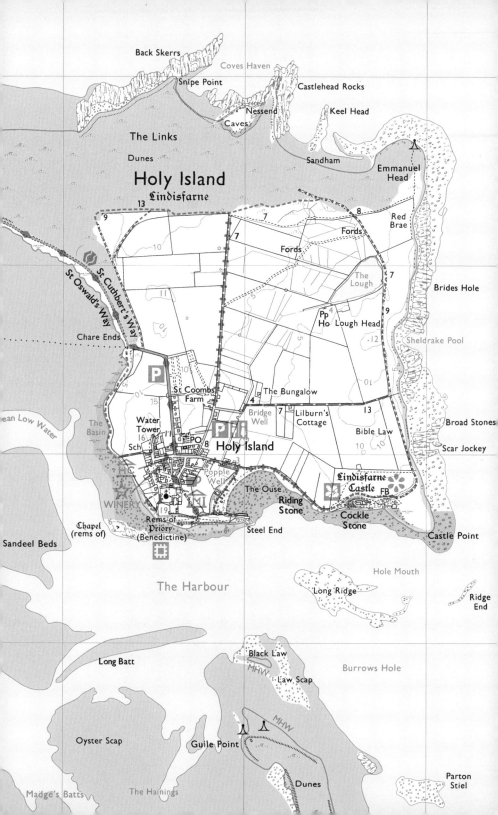

Back Skerrs

Coves Haven

Snipe Point

Castlehead Rocks

Nessend

Keel Head

Caves

The Links

Sandham

Emmanuel
Head

Dunes

Holy Island
Lindisfarne

13

9

7

7

8

Red
Brae

7

Fords

Fords

The
Lough

7

10

11

Pp
Ho

Lough Head

9

Brides Hole

Sheldrake Pool

12

St Cuthbert's Way

St Oswald's Way

Chare Ends

10

The Bungalow

P

4

The Basin

15

St Coombs
Farm

Bridge
Well

7

Lilburn's
Cottage

13

Broad Stones

ean Low Water

Water
Tower

16

P

Bible Law

Scar Jockey

Sch

PO

8

Holy Island

3

10

The
Basin

Popple
Well

The Ouse

Lindisfarne
Castle

FB

WINERY

19

Rems of
Priory
(Benedictine)

Chapel
(rems of)

Steel End

Riding
Stone

Cockle
Stone

Castle Point

Sandeel Beds

The Harbour

Hole Mouth

Long Ridge

Ridge
End

Long Batt

Black Law

MHW

Burrows Hole

Law Scap

Oyster Scap

Guile Point

MHW

Madge's Batts

The Hainings

Dunes

Parton
Stiel

$\mathcal{M}ap$ 9 HADRIAN'S WALL

'The Roman Empire first became interested in Britain in the first century BC,' Aunt Bea declared. We were standing in the ancient fort of Vercovicium, looking out across the rolling scenery of Cumbria in the astonishing landscape of the Northumberland National Park. 'Julius Caesar was the first emperor to seriously invade us, in 55 BC. Invasion after invasion followed, because empires always need enemies to crush. It took them until 84 AD to bring what would become England and Wales under full imperial control as the province of Britannia. They were never able to take Scotland – the Caledonii were too fierce, and the land too forbidding – though they got within a mile at Bowness-on-Solway in Cumbria.'

I thought of the steep hills we'd passed through earlier in our trip, the roads winding through stone and dark forest, and their wolves and the deep lochs, and said I could well believe it.

'Yes, quite. After a while, a fairly new emperor, Hadrian, claimed to have had a divine vision regarding the importance of keeping his empire intact. Nothing would do but a great big wall had to be built across the north of Britannia, with manned forts every mile along its length. Construction started around 122 and finished by 130. It's estimated that it took 15,000

men to complete its 73 miles. There are theories and theories as to why. It certainly wasn't necessary on defensive grounds. I think he just wanted to show off, honestly. New to the job, unrest on many frontiers, lots of rivals looking for advantage... Well, I mean, a huge white wall right across the island is quite the statement, particularly for a culture that prided itself on its engineering accomplishments. When an emperor decides they need to build a wall, it's normally more about saying something to the people inside it, than to those on the other side.' She winked at me.

'Now, after we solve this lot of clues, I fancy a hamburger. Can you look up somewhere to get one on your phone?'

▨ Easy

1. How many times does the word TURRET appear on the map?

2. The impressive roman fort of Vercovicium, known now as Housesteads after a local farm, was built for which Roman emperor?

▨ Medium

3. Can you find three different names on the map that sound as if they might be warm?

4. Is Bradley closer to Kennel Crags or East Morwood?

▨ Tricky

5. In total, how many springs and wells are indicated on the map?

6. Can you find out which of the national trails shown on the map is the longest overall?

▨ Challenging

7. Despite the common misconception, Hadrian's Wall has never marked the border between England and Scotland. Can you discover the name of the most river-like of rivers that separated England from Scotland at its narrowest point?

8. Can you reassemble the following fragments to find four words printed on the map? ADS, ATE, BEG, CUL, GA, HO, ION, NG, OG, RB, STA, STE, TI, USE, VAT

> ### Key Puzzle
> * What is the designation of Greenlee Lough?

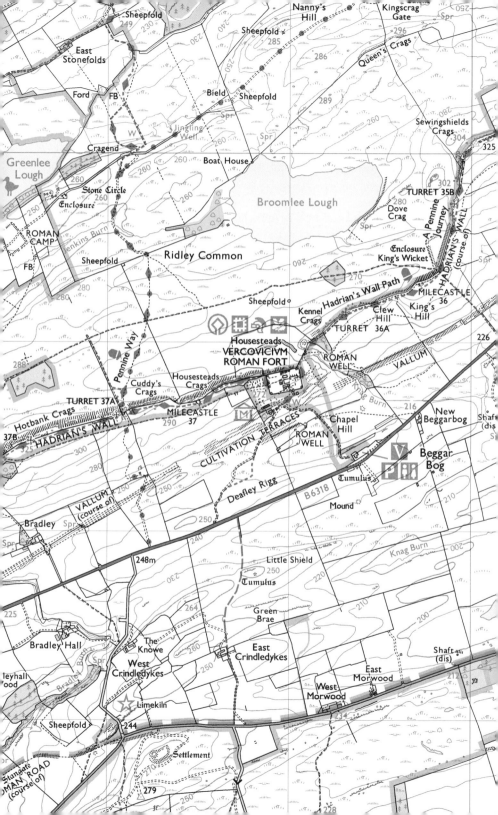

Map 10 ST BEES

Standing at the tip of St Bees Head on a clear day, looking west towards Ireland, you can see the Isle of Man. It's a fierce sort of place, with gorse and thick grass toughened by the wind that comes off the Irish Sea tufting on the clifftop. Birds wheel above us and Aunt Bea is excited because in among the herring gulls and fulmars she wants to see the guillemots.

It is, according to Aunt Bea, as far west as you can get in northern England.

'The trip we've just taken, from Lindisfarne to St Bees, the far east to the far west of England, is pretty much the narrowest width of any point on the whole island and packed full of history. There have been people living here for more than 5,000 years; they've found evidence of Mesolithic settlement and who knows who came before that but left no trace.'

We stood up by the white lighthouse on the north head, feeling out on the edge of the world.

We strolled down the cliff, into St Bees village, and watched the walkers with their dogs on the long beach. She pointed out to sea, where above the haze coming off the sea, I could see what looked like mountains rising out of the water.

'Just under 200 miles that way, it's the Isle of Man, which among many other things famously proves John Donne wrong that no man is an island. Another 90-odd miles south/south-west and you hit Ireland.'

She turned her back to the sea, pointing her arm back inland.

'About 20 miles that way, as the guillemot flies, is St Oswald's Church, where Wordsworth is buried. If we were to travel south, the next land we'd hit would be the north coast of Wales. There's a walk that starts, or ends here, called the Wainwright Coast to Coast Walk. It takes you from the Irish Sea to the North Sea, 182 miles, crossing through the Lake District, the Yorkshire Dales and the North York Moors and ending up in Robin Hood's Bay. It's always been on my list. Almost 400 acres of the area have been marked as being of special scientific interest, the head is designated as a stretch of heritage coast, and, of course, there's the reserve. The cliffs aren't especially ancient, but the local sandstone is unusually fine. Any or all of that could be part of why we're here.'

She turned back to the sea again.

'Or none of it. It might just be that our mysterious guide wanted to show us something lovely. I'm sure we'll figure it out tonight. I've booked us rooms above a pub with a particularly snug bar. We can sit and puzzle out our next steps as we wait for dinner.'

■ Easy

1. Which location on the map sounds split in two?

2. What elevation is the tallest triangulation pillar on the map?

■ Medium

3. Can you find a palindromic upland?

4. Which three location names include words generally associated with birds?

■ Tricky

5. What creatures are protected at the St Bees Head nature reserve?

6. One contour line encloses, against a map border, a triangulation pillar and a shepherd's pen, but not a Hall. What is its elevation?

■ Challenging

7. Can you find locations on the map that are anagrams of the following words or phrases? Ignore the spaces and punctuation, which may differ from those in the place names.
   a. RAVEN BLOTCH   b. TOTALLING NORTH
   c. MY ARTFUL PRO   d. CROWBAR SALE

8. Can you discover how St Bees Head got its name?

⚲ Key Puzzle

* What name is shown a short way to the north-west of the pub?

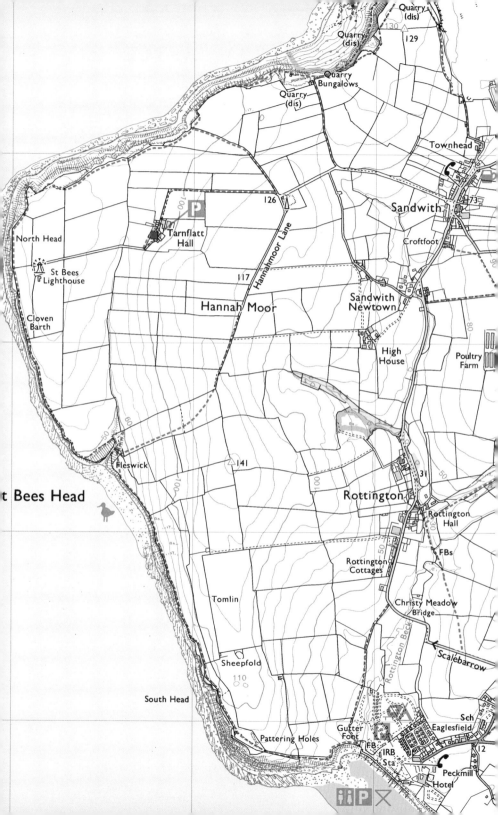

Map II WRAY CASTLE

Aunt Bea drove us through the winding roads of the Lake District and on to our next destination, Windermere.

'You'll forgive me if I go the scenic route, so we can come in through Coniston,' she called above the engine.

I was dozing and started awake.

'Sorry, dear boy, but you won't want to miss the Old Man.' Or at least I think that's what she said.

The Old Man turned out to be a high fell that loomed over a beautiful narrow lake, which looked magical as the early morning mist lifted from it. As we left that behind, coming almost immediately upon another, even bigger lake, I turned to Aunt Bea. She cut me off.

'You were about to say there are a lot of lakes in the Lake District, weren't you?'

I knew that Windermere was going to be beautiful. It's practically the poster child for the whole Lake District. But it's one thing to know that, and another to see it for yourself. We got out of the car and stood there for a long time, watching the water shift and change as the day brightened.

'You can see why the Romantics were obsessed with it here, can't you? It's a beautiful balance between wildness and cultivation. Just the right amount of danger lurking at the edges to make you feel you've been somewhere proper. You can see how a young Beatrix Potter might have been inspired by that mix of the wild and the human. Fir and tweed, nature red in tooth and claw and bonnets. You can almost see Peter bounding around the corner in his blue jacket with Mr McGregor in hot pursuit can't you? She came back here throughout her young life, and when her writing career took off she bought land all across the Lake District. At the time of her death she donated some 4,000 acres to the National Trust. But the first time she came here was to Wray Castle,' she told me, as we set out on our walk.

'Very imposing, it is. All crenulations and buttresses and cruciform arrow slits and rigidly straight lines, rendered in heavy grey stone. Perfect for repelling enemy knights. It's all a lie, of course. The arrow slits don't even go anywhere. It was built in 1840 for a surgeon who had a rich wife, and it's perfectly pleasant inside. It's very convincing though, a great example of the Victorian Gothic. Perhaps the lesson here is not to take things at face value – or not to put too much faith in the things that the world presents as true. So be on the lookout for trickery and deception, my boy. Particularly when on a treasure hunt!'

QUESTIONS

■ Easy

1. How many sheepfolds are there on the map?

2. How might you approach Low Wray from the east differently in summer than in winter?

■ Medium

3. What is the highest number written in orange on the map?

4. What might be the smelliest place on the map?

■ Tricky

5. Sum the numbers of the two highest A-roads together, and subtract the number of the B-road. Halve the result, and add the number of times the word 'Brathay' appears on the map. Divide by the number of ferry routes out of Ecclerigg House, and find the resulting number in black. Heading directly west, how many contour lines do you cross before leaving the map?

6. Blelham Tarn, with its associated bogland, is a site of special scientific interest. What is a tarn?

■ Challenging

7. What is the name and species of the famous Beatrix Potter antagonist who links Crag and Hole on the map?

8. Which of the following words is the odd one out?
   a. Angle   b. Brathay
   c. Gale   d. Pull

Key Puzzle

* There are several churches on the map, but only one ecclesiastical word. What is it?

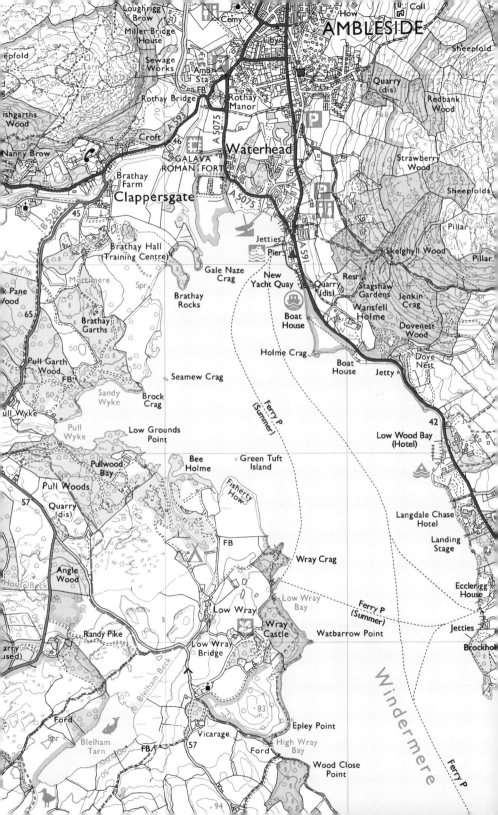

Map 12 WHITBY ABBEY

'Ours is not to reason why. We go where the clues lead, my boy!'

I had expressed barely the smallest murmur of complaint that we were traversing the whole width of the country again to head for the north-eastern coast.

'But what a route, my boy. We'll leave the Lake District, bisect the North Pennines and the Yorkshire Dales and clip the North York Moors, before we arrive at our destination. Three of our most attractive national parks and one area of outstanding natural beauty in one trip. Not bad at all.' As she described the formation of the Pennines, I let my eyelids droop for a moment.

'What leaps to mind when you think of Whitby?' Aunt Bea didn't wait for me to answer. 'Is it poetry?'

I admitted that it was not.

'Vampires then?'

I looked at her.

'Well, we know that it was in Whitby that Bram Stoker first learned of Vlad the Impaler. He would have seen the bats flitting about at night, the graves splitting where the clifftop graveyard was eroding. Of course, when he comes to write the novel and the count is shipwrecked just off the coast, it's here he comes to…'

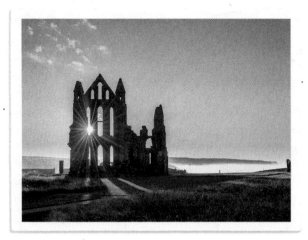

At that moment, just as the sun was beginning to dip, we came upon the ruined abbey, which looked spectacular framed against the sky with the red roofs of the town scattered out beneath it.

Aunt Bea lowered her voice. 'Another monastery sacked by the Vikings in the ninth century and then again by Henry VIII during the Reformation.'

We watched as the sky lit orange behind the stones, the shadows in the arched window frames suddenly darkening.

'It should be poetry, too. The first English poet we know of, Cædmon, lived and worked at the abbey here in the seventh century. He looked after the animals until a divine dream taught him the art of verse. St Hilda promptly enrolled him as a monk, and his work became a source of religious inspiration right across the country. Almost all of his poetry has been lost now, sadly. Mysteries upon mysteries, my boy. This country is layered with them. Now, is there enough light left to read those clues?'

Easy

1. What is the name of the famous vampire associated with Whitby?

2. Which location name, derived from a local stream, appears twice on the map?

Medium

3. Which location might have the most valuable trees?

4. Which saint is associated with Whitby's best-known tourist attraction?

Tricky

5. Which of these words is the odd one out?
   a. Castle   b. Hill
   c. Lodge   d. Manor
   e. Mill

6. How many different numbered roads are labelled on the map?

Challenging

7. Can you discover the precise age in years of the town's traditional ceremony that takes place annually during Holy Week? The total 15 will be useful to you here.

8. From a cicatrix location, follow a recreational route west and south to the edge of a farm and, from there, to the nearest place of worship. Head north-east, and you'll pass slightly north of a peak. How tall is it?

Key Puzzle

* Where is there a school with a recreation centre?

Map 13 HUMBER BRIDGE

After a couple of hours curving down the north-eastern coast we reached the mouth of the River Humber and turned inland. You get a wonderful view of the Humber Bridge from the cliff at Hessle. It's almost a mile and a half long, the road suspended from powerful cables that run from pillar to pillar.

'They say that 120,000 vehicles a week cross the Humber here,' Aunt Bea said. She sounded thoughtful. 'It took them nine years to build it, and they'd been planning a crossing for 40 years before that. It was the longest suspension bridge in the world for nearly 20 years, and, even now, there are only 10 others longer. The bridge cut 50 miles off the journey distance between Hull and Grimsby, as well as alleviating a whole swathe of horrible traffic congestion right across the region.' She looked at me expectantly.

'That's good,' I said.

'Good?'

'Yeah, I mean, improving the traffic between Hull and Grimsby – it's hardly Vikings sacking an ancient monastery or the birthplace of English poetry, is it?'

'You listen here, my boy. Don't let the fact that humans have made magic ordinary blind you.'

She pointed at the imposing bridge stretching across the river, the two towers like ladders climbing into the sky.

Humber Bridge

'This is a massively impressive feat of British engineering. It took two years just to wind those huge cables, and it reshaped the region. Never fall into the fallacy that the past is automatically more important than now. An understanding of the past informs what we do now. What we do will become history. How to make life more pleasant and convenient, escaping the confines of what came before, that's what we've always been doing as a species. Who knows, this could be here in a hundred years when some distant descendant is on a similar journey to ours. Something to bear in mind. Whether our guide intended that as a message or not, I don't know. Perhaps he or she just really likes bridges. Now onwards to more clues!'

▨ Easy

1. The Humber Bridge was the longest suspension bridge in the world for 17 years. In which century was it constructed?

2. Which Hall is shown on the map?

▨ Medium

3. Which road might you take if you needed to obtain a coarse mix of sand and small stone from a quarry?

4. What is the number of the European long-distance path which one of the recreational routes named on the map is part of?

▧ Tricky

5. How many living creatures are pictured on the map?

6. The Humber Bridge connects which British ceremonial counties? To be precise here, it may be useful to develop SARKY THEORIES and a NEON CORNISH THRILL.

▨ Challenging

7. What words printed on the map mean:
   a. cape   b. marauder
   c. puppies   d. safe place
   e. swampy meadows

8. Count the number of buildings on the map that are both north of the A15 and west of the A164. Find where this number appears furthest south on the map. There is a contour line near it. Follow that line west to a scrubby outcropping. Head directly north from the centre of that outcropping. What is the last printed letter you pass through before leaving the map, and what colour is it?

🔍 Key Puzzle

* Which word is closest to the south-west corner of the map?

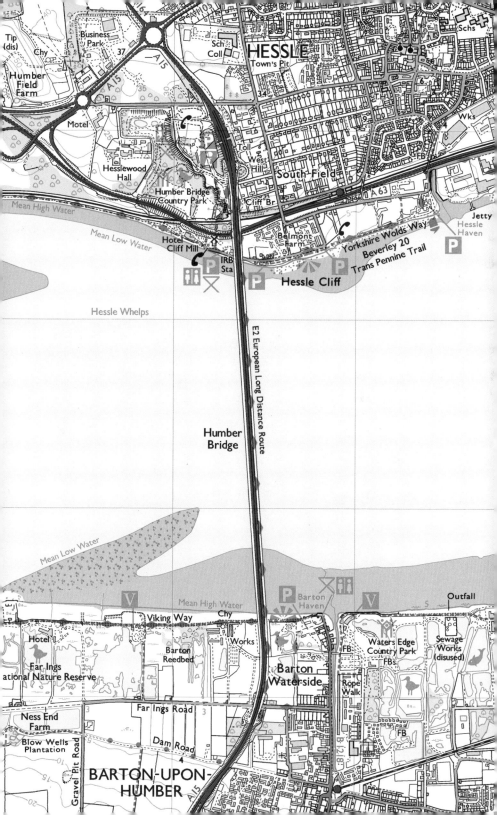

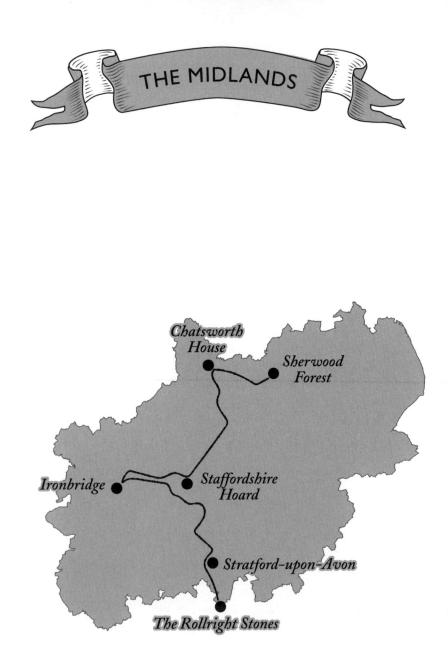

THE MIDLANDS

Chatsworth House

Sherwood Forest

Ironbridge

Staffordshire Hoard

Stratford-upon-Avon

The Rollright Stones

NORTH SEA

ENGLISH
CHANNEL

Map 14 SHERWOOD FOREST

We left the coast and turned inland.

Going from somewhere created entirely by mankind to a place that has been wooded since antiquity made for a fascinating contrast. Sherwood Forest is everything you'd hope it would be, a huge expanse of birches and oaks, mixed in with heaths and grasslands. According to the visitor centre, there are over 1,000 oaks that are more than 500 years old, and the forest has a greater concentration of ancient trees than anywhere else in Europe.

We walked for several hours under the trees.

'There's something about oak trees, my boy. They speak to us. The country was covered in oak forests 5,000 years ago. It was oak that built the wells that first allowed us to farm. One of the earliest human carvings ever found is in oak. The druids were worshipping in oak groves when the Romans arrived. It was oak beams that first held up parliament. Oak hulls carried Cook on the HMS *Endeavour* and Nelson on the HMS *Victory*. It was oak struts that held the earth up as men hacked coal to power the Industrial Revolution.' She picked up an acorn. 'The greatest oaks have been little acorns.'

Of course, you can't even really think about Sherwood Forest without considering Robin Hood.

'I'm not talking about the sanitised cartoon version, green hat and tights, all that nonsense. Hood was already told as a legend by 1380 or so,' Aunt Bea said. 'There's a clear reference to people telling stories about him in a medieval poem called *Piers Plowman*. Just 20 years later, we have another poem, *Friar Daw's Reply*, that claims "Many men speak of Robin Hood but never shot his bow" as a common proverb. Unfortunately, neither source quotes any of the actual stories told about him at the time. Our earliest actual story is from around 1450, by which time who knows.' She gestured at the enormous, ancient Major Oak in front of us.

Even the posts supporting many of the larger branches seem to add to the effect, as if it were an old man bent low with a walking stick. You can easily see why people decided it had to be Robin Hood's original base. It's thought to be as much as a thousand years old too, so the timing would work. Just think, when Richard I was setting sail to begin the Third Crusade, this tree would have been already over a hundred years old.

'So much is forgotten,' she said. 'Time makes liars of us all.'

QUESTIONS

Easy

1. Who was Robin Hood's primary lieutenant?

2. What is the elevation of the highest ground survey point on the map?

Medium

3. Can you find two locations on the map whose names reference astronomical bodies?

4. What is the official name for the period Sherwood Forest dates from?

Tricky

5. Head east from a Plantation that sounds like it should have a Tower, to the tip of a triangle. Heading north from there will take you to a track. Turn right onto the track and then, sticking to tracks, take a left, another left, a right, another right, a left, and then the third right. And keep going to a crossroads. What location is a short distance to your north-west?

6. The tales of Robin Hood are commonly held to be set in which century?

Challenging

7. Can you find locations that sound like the following:
   a. the heart of the forest
   b. a stand of trees where there is more to be witnessed
   c. a location to store clothes
   d. a place where multiple trimmed rocks meet

8. Can you discover which location on the map shares its name with a district of Buenos Aires in Argentina?

Key Puzzle

* What is the alternative name of the spot said to be Robin Hood's bower? It may help you to imagine a tree that could move any number of unoccupied squares, in a straight line vertically, horizontally or diagonally.

Map 15 CHATSWORTH HOUSE

Far from the wild ancient woodland we had just left, the carefully manicured grounds surrounding Chatsworth House felt like a very different England. We stood on a bridge over the River Derwent gazing over the beautiful grounds.

'They just feel different, don't they, these beech trees? They're still old, eighteenth-century some of them. And these woods have been here in one form or another since medieval times. And there's been an estate here since the eleventh century, though the majority of what we see here is far later, of course. I have to admit to an inordinate fondness for baroque architecture, and why not when it's this lovely? They say the window frames catch the light like that because of gold leaf.'

We walked along the curving path to the house as tourists took pictures.

'There's a special aura to a place that has been steeped in power and wealth for more than 500 years, all in the ownership of the same family.'

After a period of contemplation, and some cross-referencing with our map of the immediate area, Aunt Bea turned to me.

'Every great house is a palimpsest, a parchment that has been written and rewritten, time and again. Inside and out, Chatsworth's magnificence is rooted in sympathetic revision. The Cavendish family have altered many things over the centuries, but never carelessly. Even when there has been significant damage to repair, as after the Civil War, the work undertaken has been with one foot in the future, but one also in the past. The same impulse as planting an oak tree, so your descendants might enjoy its shade. It is, you might say, a bridge through time, even though it is not a span that we can cross.' She shot me an amused glance. 'That is probably for the best.'

QUESTIONS

■ Easy

1. How many times does the word 'Park' appear on the map?

2. According to the map, what does Maud possess?

■ Medium

3. What do 'Over', 'Nether' and 'Far' have in common?

4. How many weirs would you go through if you boated along the stretch of the River Derwent shown on the map?

■ Tricky

5. Which location on the map could be a thicket of bric-a-brac?

6. Chatsworth House has been repeatedly chosen as one of Britain's best stately homes. Which National Park is it in? It is the perfect place to hang a painting once you have the ARTIST PICKED.

■ Challenging

7. Find a rock especially suitable for a 50th anniversary. There is a contour line that passes through its final consonant. Follow it south until you reach the next consonant it intersects with. Travel west until you pass just north of an animal. Turn southwards until you reach a pleasant shady place. Who is traditionally said to have exercised there?

8. What would you find at the highest point shown on the map, and where is it located?

🔍 Key Puzzle

* How many places named 'End' appear on the map?

Map 16 STAFFORDSHIRE HOARD

'Occasionally, my boy, we get lucky and stumble on some genuinely significant history preserved down through the centuries. It still happens, even now. For all our clever technology and aerial surveillance, and our legions of historians and archaeologists and researchers, there's no accounting for luck. There truly are all manner of lost wonders waiting out there to be found, hidden under the ground, or long forgotten in the cavernous storerooms of museums and libraries.'

I pointed out that if that were not the case, our quest would seem a little pointless.

'And they are not to be found trapped behind the amber of a screen but out and about "IRL" as I believe you youngsters say. A man and his metal detector recently found a piece of gold in a newly ploughed field. They eventually found thousands of objects. Gold, silver, garnets. A window back to the seventh century when Christianity was beginning to spread. They think that such a treasure must have belonged to an important warrior,

perhaps even a member of the royal household. The hoard is stored now jointly in Birmingham Museum and in Stoke-on-Trent in the Potteries Museum.'

'So why have the clues sent us to a field just off the A5?' I asked.

'Well, that's all part of it. While the notebook that is guiding us includes some quite modern wonders, the notes inside make it clear that the areas were steps along the way beforehand, too. Where there's a bridge, there's an ancient fording place. So it could be the famous treasure that brings us this way but it could as easily be Watling Street, one of the most important old ways across Britain. Its origins are pre-Roman, although we're a bit far north for that section, and there are legends of goblin fairs taking place on nights of the full moon at certain specific crossroads along the route. So it is important to retain an open mind as well as a keen eye. On this sort of journey, you never know the precise significance of what you're looking at. There's often treasures hidden all around us.'

Easy

1. Where on the map is it most likely to be dusk?

2. How many bridges run above the train line?

Medium

3. Which location printed on the map carries the definite article?

4. Watling Street ends in Shropshire, but can you find out where it begins? You will need to find a cathedral in the garden of England.

Tricky

5. Which numbered road reaches the highest altitude on the map? Look for the ELEGY STORY.

6. Divide the highest A-road number printed on the map by the lowest. Divide the result by the number of the motorway shown, then subtract the largest orange number shown. What is the result?

Challenging

7. Can you discover the year in which a major Anglo-Saxon treasure hoard was found on this map? The total 11 will help you here.

8. Can you find locations on the map that are anagrams of the following words or phrases? Ignore the spaces and punctuation, which may differ from those in the place names.
   a. ANGELS TWITTER   b. CLARIFIED HOLD
   c. ALIEN WATCHER   d. OUTGROWN BENDER

Key Puzzle

* Which area is north of a farm that sounds as if it might produce fruit?

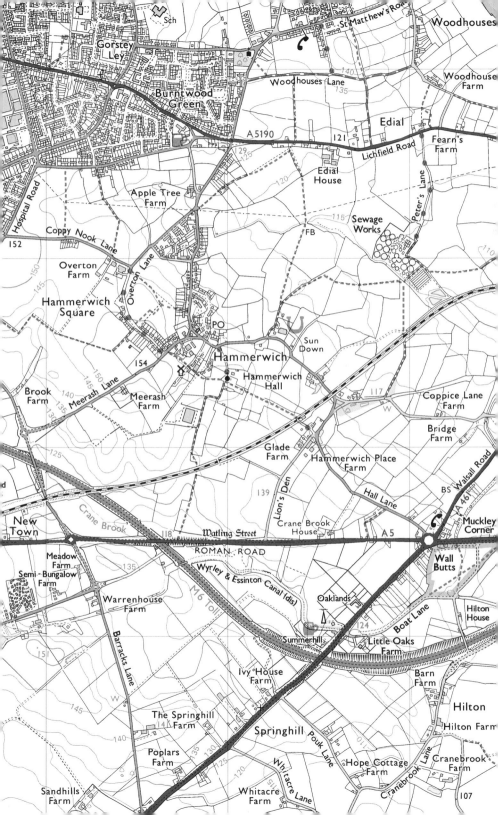

Map 17 IRONBRIDGE

We were standing on the Iron Bridge, looking across the River Severn at the slopes of Ironbridge Gorge. I'd noticed, on this journey, that some bridges felt quite light and airy despite their huge mass. The Iron Bridge, however, felt as solid as the surrounding hills. It has been standing there for close to 250 years, and it gives every impression of being prepared to stay another 250, and then 2,000 more after that, just for good measure. 'Strong bones', a local had said to us. She'd not been wrong.

'Maybe whoever hid the treasure just really likes bridges,' I said.

Breaking a period of silent contemplation, Aunt Bea said, 'This is not just a lovely spot, it's where the Industrial Revolution really got kick-started.' She pointed over the north end of the bridge, past the church and the forested hillside. 'Coalbrookdale, just over there. A fiendishly clever chap called Abraham Darby the Elder discovered that you could use coal coke to make iron. It had much better purity than iron made with normal coal, and it was a much cheaper process than using charcoal. So, in 1709, Darby's iron went out into the world, and it gave Britain a significant leg up in the process of industrialisation. Within 40 years, the first steam engine was made to power a water pump. A revolution powered by iron, coal and innovation, which changed the world forever. All those iron rails, those steam trains, those factories. Who knows how things would have been different without Abraham. His grandson was involved in making the bridge we're standing on, some 65 years later. The first ever iron bridge. If you want to consider the history of our nation over the last 300 years, this is as critical a place to stand as any you're likely to find. Besides, the view's not bad either.'

Easy

1. Which location on the map shares a name with a very important British palace and abbey?

2. What tourist and leisure facility is shown as being available in Ironbridge?

Medium

3. If you were to walk from the most southerly point of Lloyd's Coppice shown on the map to the most northerly, how much higher up would you be?

4. Which location might seem well suited to brothers?

Tricky

5. From the most westerly of three nearby mounds, head through a feminine woodland to the A4169. Turn right, then take the first left, and continue to the second contour line. Follow that east to a B-road. What is that road's number?

6. What feature shown on the map, which dates to 1779, was the first of its kind in the world and is now a UNESCO World Heritage Site?

Challenging

7. Can you find locations on the map that are anagrams of the following words or phrases? Ignore the spaces and punctuation, which may differ from those in the place names.
   a. MOCKING DONUTS
   b. THREE PEALED
   c. APACE PICNIC SPOT
   d. LEADEN LOG

8. Coneybury Farm is to the east of Broseley. What is a coneybury?

> **Key Puzzle**
> * Which road runs past Oldpark Farm?

Map 18 STRATFORD-UPON-AVON

'Out, out, brief candle!
Life's but a walking shadow, a poor player,
That struts and frets his hour upon the stage,
And then is heard no more. It is a tale
Told by an idiot, full of sound and fury,
Signifying nothing.'

Aunt Bea realised I'd walked away to stare intently at the map I was holding.

'Sorry. Couldn't resist. You know I've always thought Shakespeare's writing is kind of like a map that helps us find ourselves. Generation after generation it helps us set a course. Ah, Stratford. Cradle and grave of the Bard.' We'd taken rooms in a beautiful and deeply atmospheric Elizabethan hotel the night before, and Aunt Bea was clearly in a particularly expansive mood.

I felt much the same way, honestly. Stratford's heritage is such an important part of its identity; it has a historic feel that you don't often find. And with Aunt Bea reciting speeches and poems every time she was reminded, I felt truly immersed in the world of Shakespeare.

'There's so much of importance here. We'll have to pay particular attention to our clues and questions, and make sure we don't get led astray.'

I nodded, but Aunt Bea was just warming up.

'Take just the buildings associated with Shakespeare, for example – the house on Henley Street where he was born, his mother's home at Palmer's Farm, his father's family home at Snitterfield, the cottage in Shottery where his wife lived, and of course New Place, the great man's own home, where he died. There's a school he is thought to have attended, and a pub that was open during his time, and either could potentially be vitally formative for a writer. Or there's Holy Trinity Church, where he was baptised, attended services, got married and was finally buried. Truth be told, there's barely a square yard in the place that wouldn't have some historical significance. But then, he is our national poet, and the world's greatest playwright. Everywhere you turn in our language, you see his footprints. Is it any surprise if the same is true of the town he loved?'

Easy

1. How many times does Shakespeare's name appear on the map?

2. What height is the contour line that passes through the name 'Clopton' three times?

Medium

3. Which location could be a secret bus route?

4. Where on the map can you find a circle with three straight roads leading from it, all of them uncoloured?

Tricky

5. Add the values of the highest-numbered A- and B-roads together. Break the result into two halves, and add those halves together as if they were separate numbers. Take the result, and find a point on the map where a number appears that is within 1 of it. What name is the nearest to that point?

6. Can you discover the date that William Shakespeare's last direct descendant died? The total 14 will be useful to you here.

Challenging

7. Which locations on the map mention the following:
   a. a fairy
   b. a flower
   c. an item of clothing
   d. a man's first name
   e. a religious title
   f. a vegetable

8. Can you discover to whom the Obelisk is dedicated?

Key Puzzle

* What is the name of the footpath that runs along part of the north bank of the Avon?

Map 19 ROLLRIGHT STONES

It's easy to miss the Rollright Stones if you don't know they're there. The road they lie on is small, and runs along a ridge, while the nearby main road plunges from one valley to the next. But there's a small lay-by for parking and, over the road, a section of iron railing on the other side of a hedge marks the single King Stone. This side of the road, an unobtrusive gate leads you to a modest shack, and once you walk past that, you're suddenly in the middle of a circle of ancient, weather-beaten stones with countryside rolling off in the distance, and a thicket of trees at one end to give the place a sense of intimacy. Even Aunt Bea lowered her voice.

'These are made from Jurassic limestone. Much younger and softer than the Lewisian Gneiss at Callanish. Made from compressed sediment, possibly from an enormous lake. You can't see it on the standing stones, because of the lichen, but there are newer hunks of it placed around the area and you can see fossils. But these stones have hung on.'

We walked between the three sites and Aunt Bea unpacked their history, from the lone King Stone, the circle of the King's Men and the nearby cairn of the five Whispering Knights taking us from almost 6,000 years ago at the beginning of the Neolithic through to the middle of the Bronze Age 4,500 years later.

'There are so many legends that have sprung up around these stones. There's a sense of magic to the Rollright Stones as deep as the legends of the witchcraft that brought them into being. It's easy to imagine witchcraft here, and in fact you can sometimes find the remains of pagan and wiccan rituals left scattered around – scraps of colourful cloth, bits of crystal, pools of candle wax and other occult offerings.

'We're not far here from the old road between Stratford and London. I'd like to think that at least some of Shakespeare's fairies and witches sprang from these stones "Full fathom five thy father lies; Of his bones are coral made".'

With that we began to walk back up to where the car was parked. Somehow, nowhere else we visited on our journey was quite like those silent stones.

Easy

1. Which path is named after a famous playwright?

2. What ground survey height is listed on the longest stretch of straight road on the map?

Medium

3. What is the first general feature north of the highest point on the map?

4. What tourist and leisure facility lies between farms with 'North' and 'South' in their names?

Tricky

5. According to legend, how many stones make up the King's Men circle of the Rollright Stones? Bear in mind the answer could cause confusion on whether there is less or fewer stones remaining.

6. Can you pair up the following words to make four words printed on the map? DOWN, HILL, MILL, NORTH, PIKE, RAIL, TURN, WAY, WIND

Challenging

7. What is the elevation of the contour line that passes through the names of four farms?

8. Can you discover whether it is possible to see the village of Long Compton from the King Stone of the Rollright Stones?

Key Puzzle

* Which farm is nearest the Whispering Knights?

WALES TO
EAST ENGLAND

Conwy Suspension
Bridge

Caernarfon
Castle

Portmeirion

The Broads

University
of Cambridge

Strumble
Head

Sutton Hoo

NORTH SEA

ENGLISH
CHANNEL

Map 20 STRUMBLE HEAD

A glint had come into Aunt Bea's eye when she realised where we were headed next.

'To St George's Channel,' she said. But I just stared at her blankly.

'Cymru, my boy.'

As we travelled west through the Cotswolds, then down to cross the Severn, north of Bristol, I dozed for who knows how long until Aunt Bea nudged me awake.

'Almost there.'

I yawned and stretched. We walked out onto the cliffs from the small car park and down towards a small suspension bridge.

'It's a lonely lighthouse, that one,' Aunt Bea said. 'All alone on St Michael's Isle, perched on a grassy rock, surrounded by sky and ocean, with just a thin spit reaching back towards Strumble Head. Lighthouses often are lonely, and some of them are bleak as well, but that's not the feel I get from Strumble Head Lighthouse. It's more hopeful to me, and gives me a sense of human resilience, of fighting back against the odds. And the countryside here is so surprising and beautiful. The water is so blue. Those jagged cliffs with the waves crashing against the rocks below.'

It certainly felt dramatic, with a wind coming up and clouds gathering ominously at the edges of the day.

'It's important, too. Less so now, in this new age of GPS and automation, but Strumble Head is dangerous sailing, and it's claimed a lot of ships over the centuries. Particularly with Fishguard just a few miles down the coast. That's where the last invasion of Britain occurred, in fact. Well, so far at least. I suppose you never know. Anyway, that was at Carreg Wastad Point, just a couple of miles the other side of Fishguard, in 1797. The French were trying it on again, this time under the excuse of aiding the Irish. They sent a legion of their convicts under the command of an American who hated the British. It all fell apart, of course. There's a lesson for you there. I think it would be fair to say that not everyone's goals were... fully aligned.'

I assured her I'd bear that in mind for my next invasions, and wondered, yet again, just what she'd gotten up to when she was younger.

Easy

1. How many places have 'Carreg' in their name?

2. The area shown on the map is within which county?

Medium

3. How many springs are marked on the map?

4. Can you name a type of creature that Strumble Head is known for being particularly well suited for watching?

Tricky

5. Can you work out what the Welsh word 'ynys' means?

6. The word 'Pwll' appears in several locations on the map. What does it mean?

Challenging

7. Can you find locations that fit the following?

   a. a good place for pagans

   b. a peaceful location

   c. a door for women

   d. a directional landmark that is out of place

8. From a public telephone, follow a road to a location whose full name is eight letters long. A contour line runs through the second half of that name. Find a point that is 1m higher than that line. Which is the closest offshore island visible from this vantage point?

Key Puzzle

* What word connects Meicel, Ddu and Melyn?

Map 21 PORTMEIRION

The drive up the coast was incredible, with the final hour in Snowdonia National Park especially beautiful, as steep hills covered in lichen, bracken and grasses stretched up on one side of the road and the sea crashed against the cliffs on the other. Even Aunt Bea didn't feel the need to add anything, only remarking that, though there was plenty of history to talk about on this coast, sometimes the thing to do was to simply concentrate on looking.

'I'm assuming the statement "I am not a number, I am a free man!" means nothing to you?'

I shook my head.

She seemed disappointed. 'Giant aggressive bubbles, the Lotus Seven, poison gas?'

We were sitting in the Piazza, surrounded by palm trees and rhododendrons and happily shrieking children playing in the fountain's paddling pool. Past the classical-looking colonnade, I could see buildings painted in blues, reds and yellows ranging in intensity from vivid down to the merest hint of pastel.

'No, of course not. It doesn't involve celebrities eating insects on an island. Well, as you can see the plant life here really is quite extraordinary – they've been planting unusual species here since the Victorians, including a remarkable variety of Himalayan flowering trees and even some giant redwoods,' she continued.

'Portmeirion was always a hotel at its heart,' Aunt Bea gestured at the gorgeous, colourful village around us, 'but that does not change its importance in the slightest.'

It was as if we'd been transported to another country entirely. Off to the right, a gigantic chessboard with life-sized pieces stood apparently mid-game. I wasn't sure which side was winning.

'The designer and architect, Sir Clough Williams-Ellis, was something of a visionary. He passionately opposed the destructive modernisation of the countryside. His playful and often slightly surreal work here at Portmeirion reminded the architects of Britain that just because something was new, that didn't mean it had to be some squared-off concrete monstrosity. After the war, the village was the perfect response to the new, excited spirit of the 1960s. Postmodernism just would not have been the same without it. We owe him a significant debt.'

She tapped the notebook in front of us.

'It's time we found out where we're heading next.'

QUESTIONS

Easy

1. How many train stations are marked on the map?

2. What is the highest air survey point shown on the map?

Medium

3. Where on the map might Lincolnshire Freemasons pause?

4. What is the longest location name on the map?

Tricky

5. Find somewhere to park closest to the business park. Travel south until you reach an island. What makes the footpath to and from the island difficult to use?

6. Portmeirion was designed in the 1920s as a lovely example of a village in the style of which country's Riviera?

Challenging

7. From the most southerly church on the map, follow a road to a bridge over a river. Head downstream to the bridge-after-next, and head north to a blue letter. The same letter appears again, to the west. From the feature that letter identifies, go directly north. At the second road you come to, turn right. What do you arrive at?

8. What is the sum total of all the numbers printed on the map?

Key Puzzle

* Castelldeudraeth is now a hotel, but what was it recorded as in the twelfth century?

Map 22 CAERNARFON CASTLE

Caernarfon Castle is everything you want a medieval castle to be – powerful and imposing, with thick, arrow-slitted walls topped with crenulations and battlements. There was originally a Roman fortification in a similar spot, bounded by the River Seiont and the Menai Strait.

It's large too, and I imagined what it must have been to be an attacker looking up at those walls. There's not much left inside now, but then again, apparently no one has attacked it since the 1650s. Walls were built around the medieval town at the same time as the castle was being constructed, the end of the thirteenth century and the start of the fourteenth, and they too have mostly survived. There was a lot to see apart from the castle, too.

Aunt Bea was especially sad that we wouldn't have time to take a diversion to Snowdon, which she had very fond memories of ascending.

'It's not quite Ben Nevis but still over 3,500 feet and it's incredibly beautiful. I have fond memories of swimming "sans costume" in Glaslyn, said to be the resting place of Arthur's sword Excalibur,' Aunt Bea reminisced.

'Old Caernarfon always feels a bit French to me,' she continued. We were at a café inside the old town, a map spread over the table, looking out at the castle and the town walls. 'Bastides, they called them. Purpose-built protected towns, in strategic positions. All the rage in thirteenth- and fourteenth-century France. If the French were doing it, we had to do it too, so it became popular here for a while. But military technology always moves on, and strategic pressure points shift around the landscape, and the habit died out. But if you ever get the chance to visit Andorra, do take it up. It's quite the experience. Great place to buy furniture and go skiing. Tell Lucas at the Grand you know me and he'll get you a table somewhere good.'

I shot Aunt Bea a questioning look.

'Furniture, my dear boy. I've sold a lot of furniture in Andorra. Come, we have important matters to attempt to solve.'

▣ Easy

1. Which different sport-related facilities are indicated in blue on the map?

2. What is the name of the common?

▣ Medium

3. Which is closer to Bryn Mafon – Is-Helen or the Police Station?

4. How many different well-known women's names can you find on the map?

▣ Tricky

5. Can you find out which Welsh island lies across the Menai Strait from Caernarfon?

6. Find three farms in a row, and a black number nearest the easternmost farm. Go to where that black number appears a second time on the map. What is the nearest named location?

▣ Challenging

7. Which location is one letter away from being a convenient place to hide?

8. From the most westerly pier, proceed south to a spring, and from there to a nearby peak. Note its height, and find another place on the map where that number appears. Head directly west from there, and you'll come to a place name. Where are you?

⌕ Key Puzzle

* The Welsh word 'Aber' in a place name denotes the mouth of a river. What word is it paired with in this map?

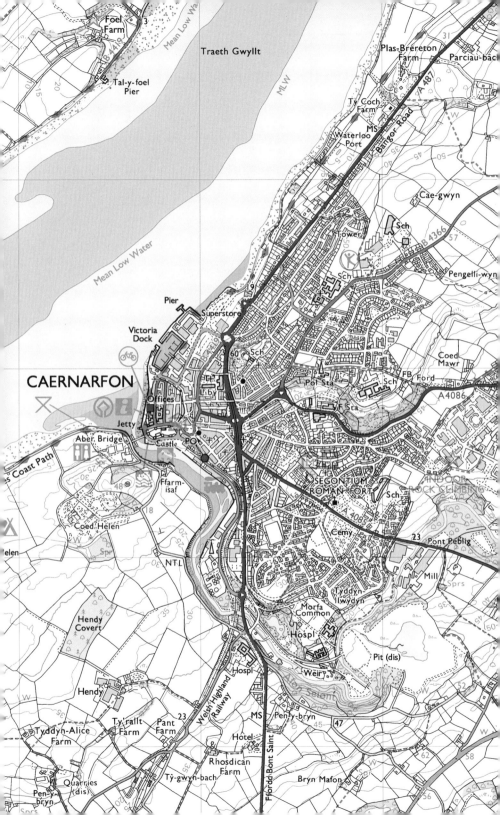

Map 23 CONWY SUSPENSION BRIDGE

Conwy Castle is nowhere near as big as Caernarfon Castle, but once Aunt Bea had pointed it out I could plainly see that they're both from the same period, with the same brooding dominance.

'There was a real statement to be made by Edward that Wales was now under English rule,' said Aunt Bea. Longshanks was over six foot tall and towered over most men at the time. He wanted his castles to do the same.

These days Conwy Castle is in significantly better shape inside than its cousin.

'That's no thanks to the previous owners,' Aunt Bea told me. 'The Earl of Conwy – there was only one – took charge of the place in 1660 and promptly stripped it of all its metal, destroying it in the process. By the nineteenth century, the castle was considered one of the loveliest ruins of Britain, a magnet for poets and painters. So when the suspension bridge was built across the river in the 1820s, it made sense to bring it right up to the old pile and run the road over its toes. I don't blame Thomas Telford, the architect, in the least. Must have made for a gorgeous route. Then the town finally got the castle back in 1865, and restoration began. The government leased it after the Second World War, and did a bunch more work, bringing it back to its current impressive condition. So now, despite the very atmospheric style of the bridgework, it does look a little like some lunatic decided to build a road almost through a medieval castle. It's a fascinating example of how environments shift, and how that changes our sense of the landscape.

Conwy Suspension Bridge

Looking on a map, you'd have no idea of the clash of eras, the change in emphasis for what we needed the land to be and do.'

She took out a map and spread it on the picnic table where we were sitting.

'The relationship between Wales and England has much darkness in its history. Much like England's relationship with Scotland, of course. But it is of eternal fascination to me, the way that the three nations have grown together and apart, the evidence of their commonalities and clashes. Tracing this story on maps and on the land. Who knows what will be next for us all?'

QUESTIONS

Easy

1. Which ruined castle is nearest The Vardre?

2. Which road runs underneath the River Conwy?

Medium

3. How many places of worship are there on the map?

4. Which UNESCO World Heritage Site is adjacent to the original Conwy Bridge?

Tricky

5. Is the library closer to Bryn Bychan or the Clubhouse?

6. Which feature shown on the map sounds like a famous Mike Oldfield album first released in 1973?

Challenging

7. Start at the southerly end of the B5106 and take the third green right of way you come to. Follow that to a yellow road. From the nearest chevron, head east to a coniferous tree marked on a light green background. Then proceed directly north until you touch the letter 'n'. What is the nearest number printed in black?

8. Conwy is home to a location identified by the *Guinness Book of Records* as holding a British record. Can you discover what that record is?

Key Puzzle

* Double the value of the road that no longer runs over the Conwy Bridge, and add one more metre than the ground survey height shown north of Tywyn. What do you get?

Map 24 UNIVERSITY OF CAMBRIDGE

'Most of them hate to have to admit it.' Aunt Bea paused to make a grandiose, sweeping gesture that took in the towering buildings around us. 'But Cambridge is the offspring of Oxford. A group of Oxford scholars aggravated the townsfolk so much that they had to flee, and they chose Cambridge, making it the second-oldest English-language university, and the fourth oldest of all those still in existence, after Bologna, Oxford and Salamanca. They've been refining the place constantly for over 800 years.'

We had arrived into Cambridge after a long sweeping trip south-east through the centre of England. At the beginning of our trip, I had felt guilty that Aunt Bea was doing so much driving, but quickly I had seen that nothing made her as happy as setting off in Bertha on a new adventure, calling out some landmark as we passed it. Just past Birmingham, she got very animated and gestured at a motorway sign.

'That's the exit to take for Coton in the Elms,' she called excitedly. I looked back at her blankly.

'It's the place in Britain that's furthest from the sea! One mile south-east of Church Flatts Farm. But even then that's still only 70 miles. No distance at all really. Remember my dear boy, a nation of ferrymen!'

As we came into Cambridge from the west, the buildings started to become

ever more impressive. The university is not one piece, it's a patchwork woven through the city, and the only constants are magnificence and immaculate preservation. It's rare to find anywhere with so many centuries visibly jostling shoulder-to-shoulder. Cambridge was a fascinating place.

Aunt Bea wagged a finger at me. 'Don't be entirely taken in by the word "university". That has a very specific meaning, one that strictly begins with medieval Europe. There have been many ancient places of higher education, research and learning. Plato founded his famous academy in 387 BC, and although that's the earliest one I can think of offhand, there's every chance that older institutions existed. No disrespect to Cambridge's amazing achievements, of course. Isaac Newton, Charles Darwin, Francis Crick and James Watson. Who knows what else they'd have accomplished here, if they'd awarded women degrees before 1948. For all I know, the puzzles we need to solve here are rooted in the idea of standing on the shoulders of giants. Let's get to it, eh?'

QUESTIONS

Easy

1. Are there more farms or cemeteries identified on the map?

2. How many schools are shown in the top row of the map?

Medium

3. If you move directly from the one cycle hire location to the other as the crow flies and then keep on going, what is the height of the ground survey point you pass through?

4. How many houses run along the south side of the A1303 from the 13m ground-surveyed height point and the junction with the A1134?

Tricky

5. The names of three colleges of the University of Cambridge appear on the map as part of other location names. Can you find at least one?

6. The University of Cambridge, which was founded in 1209, is the fourth-oldest of the world's surviving universities. Can you discover which of its 31 colleges is the oldest? It will help to think of the dwelling of the one who was robbed to pay Paul.

Challenging

7. Can you discover which modern sport was first played on a common shown on this map?

8. Which of the following sports is the odd one out? Cricket, golf, punting, rugby, swimming.

Key Puzzle

* Which Way is named on the map?

THE ORDNANCE SURVEY GREAT BRITISH TREASURE HUNT

116

Map 25 THE BROADS

After regretfully deciding we didn't have time to try out punting in Cambridge, Aunt Bea finally got her way at our next destination when we got out onto the water. We were standing on the deck of a modern electric motor launch on the River Bure – 'It's pronounced "Burr", my boy, not "Bewer"' – alongside the marshes near the gorgeous village of Horning. It was a lovely day, and we were far from the only people making the most of the river. Our map of the area was laid out in front of us, and we'd been cross-referencing comments and diagrams in a dozen different notebook pages for what felt like an hour.

'Our species has always transformed the land we live on,' Aunt Bea said.

That felt like a non-sequitur, but even her most eccentric statements usually made sense at some point.

'Take the area around us, for example. The Broads is just over 300 square kilometres, the smallest National Park in the country, but to my mind, one of the most fascinating. This whole landscape is the result of human ingenuity and endeavour, of taming and exploiting and reclaiming and husbanding. In the twelfth century, this was an especially populous bit of the country and they needed fuel for their fires. They discovered that the partially decomposed matter known as peat burnt well and so began to dig it. It was hard, messy work but for 100-odd years it made sense. And then the sea levels rose, the huge holes filled with water and the "broads" were created. So what are they, "nature"? At what point does nature and mankind's influence on the landscape become the same thing? Are standing stones nature? At what point will a cathedral become natural? Does it even matter?'

I guessed this was one of those questions she didn't actually need me to answer.

'We think of our natural environment as just that, natural. But nowhere that has a long history of human occupation is entirely natural, however it may appear. It's a trivially obvious fact of life in a city, but it's every bit as true here. We transform the world around us, and yes, sometimes the result is horrible. But not always. Ancient woodland, grasslands, all formed by human hands. You need to remember that we are as capable of grace as we are of debasement. If you forget it, the world will strip away your capacity for hope and wonder, and we can't afford to be without those things. If you take nothing else from this adventure but that, then I will consider it a victory. These lines on a map, these symbols, they are a story to be teased out, the greatest story there is. Humanity.'

QUESTIONS

Easy

1. Which other county do the Norfolk Broads extend into?

2. How many public house symbols appear on the map?

Medium

3. Which named location is the lowest area on the map?

4. Where can you find a self-contained patch of access land on the map?

Tricky

5. What do the following words have in common?
   Fen, House, Shoot, Worth

6. What distinguishes the broads from natural lakes?

Challenging

7. Can you find five locations that start with birds' names? How about six more locations with other creatures somewhere in their names?

8. Find a lodging house that sounds like it would be a suitable place to rest for a meal fit for a king. A short way west, which green symbols are contained within the bowl of a water feature that looks like a champagne flute?

Key Puzzle

* Which word is less than a grid square to the east of a public house symbol?

Map 26 SUTTON HOO

Sutton Hoo is an odd sort of place name when you see it on a map. After a fair bit of coaching over the course of our trip, I could make a fair guess at 'Sutton' as possibly being a corruption of 'south town', but the Hoo was baffling. Aunt Bea congratulated me.

'You're not far off on Sutton, my boy. A village or even a single farm is more likely, but words do twist. As for the Hoo, that's from an Old English word for a high place, specifically a ridge shaped like a heel spur. So pretty much "Ridge by the South Village". A fairly unassuming name for a place that has transformed our understanding of history. We used to think of the early medieval time as a very restricted period after the Romans left, the whole myth of the "Dark Ages", but that was one of the most valuable things we discovered with the spectacular hoards here – definitive proof of a vibrant, strong, well-connected society.'

We were walking around the angular buildings to the café, ready to 'refuel' as Aunt Bea put it, before we ventured into the exhibition hall.

'Picture it, the early summer of 1939, Britain on the brink of war and Basil Brown, the self-taught archaeologist that widow Edith Pretty had personally employed, finds something, which he identifies as "an iron rivet from a medieval ship". Then he finds another. And another. Over the coming weeks, they removed earth from what they realised was a buried ship's hull. And then they found the burial chamber.'

By this point Aunt Bea was gesturing excitedly with a piece of carrot cake.

'We had always known the Roman Empire and its tendrils stretched across most of the classical world, into Africa and Asia, but we don't often think about Britain having been plugged into that network for centuries. They will have left a culture of international trade behind. Wave after wave of Germanic and Scandinavian settlers came into the east of Britain afterwards, and they brought their own traders with them as well. It seems like common sense now, but Sutton Hoo helped prove it to the naysayers who wanted to feel oh-so superior to the medieval folks. The beautiful artistry, the wealth of it all, the presence of specific materials, it all highlighted how patronising the myth of the "Dark Ages" had been. Now, let us see if we can shed some light on these clues.'

Easy

1. Which location on the map sounds the prickliest?

2. How many halls are so named on the map?

Medium

3. How many schools are shown on the map?

4. Which named Wood shown on the map takes its name from the river, whose name is not shown? The river's name has a BIRD VENEER.

Tricky

5. What do the words 'err', 'pit', 'rot' and 'ton' have in common?

6. The area shown on the map falls within which English county?

Challenging

7. Find the difference in value between the highest-numbered A-road and the highest-numbered B-road shown on the map and add twice the number of times the word 'Hoo' appears. Divide by three, and find where the resulting number is printed on the map on a green background, directly south of a farm. What is the name of that farm?

8. The treasure trove found at the Sutton Hoo ship burial site represents one of the most spectacular collections of artefacts ever found in England. Can you discover the name of the person whose land it was found on?

Key Puzzle

* What lies between a nursery and a nearby footpath?

SOUTH EAST
ENGLAND

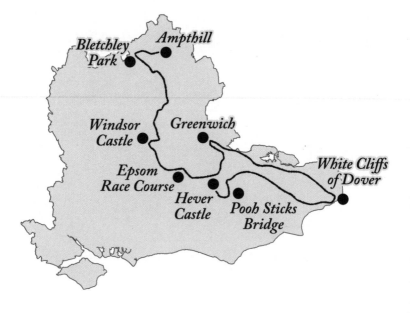

Bletchley
Park

Ampthill

Windsor
Castle

Greenwich

White Cliffs
of Dover

Epsom
Race Course

Hever
Castle

Pooh Sticks
Bridge

NORTH SEA

ENGLISH
CHANNEL

Map 27 AMPTHILL

Ampthill Park is a green and pleasant piece of lightly wooded landscaping in the rolling Bedfordshire countryside. From near the west end of the park, you can look down across the tree-fringed reservoir to where the park's formerly attached seventeenth-century house still stands.

'It's interesting that we're here,' Aunt Bea said. 'Following on from our conversation in Norfolk.' We'd been discussing vectors and triangulation, and the Millbrook Church of St Michael on the far side of the railway line, but she'd been silent for a minute or two since then.

'Does the name Capability Brown mean anything to you?' Aunt Bea asked.

'Is it a kind of rabbit?'

'Capability Brown was an extraordinary landscape architect in the eighteenth century, kind of a supercharged gardener. He would make the most extraordinary interventions to improve a landscape. Moving a hill or a forest, damming rivers to get the shape of lake he favoured, all set in those elegant hills. His style was so influential, it's come to define a certain sort of English landscape.'

She pointed out how the clumps of trees were classic Capability Brown, a kind of studied wildness that was everywhere in the grounds of these stately houses when you learned to look
for it.

'Anyway, speaking of rabbits. What about the Golden Hare?'

I must have looked unusually blank.

'Don't you know about *Masquerade?* Ah, my boy, the things you've missed. *Masquerade* was the first of the great modern treasure hunts. Written and beautifully illustrated by a fiendishly clever and subtle chap named Kit Williams, it was a series of terribly difficult clues woven through with myth and art and story that all pointed to a single spot – the spot where, at noon on the equinox, the tip of the shadow cast by that cross lands. Williams had buried the treasure, a golden sculpture of a hare, at that spot. The book was a sensation, and it has sparked countless imitators since. As I said, I find it interesting that we are here now, on our own treasure hunt.'

LUTON
& STEVENAGE
Hitchin & Ampthill

OS EXPLORER
1:25 000 scale   4 cm to 1 km – 2½ inches to 1 mile

Easy

1. How many locations named House are shown on the map?

2. Are there more wells or farms shown on the map, and by how many?

Medium

3. What is the difference between the highest point elevation shown as measured from the ground, and the highest as measured from the air?

4. Which location on the map sounds like a chunk of a back gate?

Tricky

5. What was the real first name of the famous eighteenth-century landscape architect, known as 'England's Greatest Gardener', who designed Ampthill Park? His namesake was friend to a king, lover to a queen and father to the seeker of the grail.

6. Where can you find the following words as part of longer words printed on the map?
   a. dust   b. rave   c. search   d. servo   e. stern

Challenging

7. Find a contour line that passes through a medical facility, and follow it to the eastern edge of the map. Head south–south-west to a nearby body of water, and from the tip of that proceed directly west until you reach a black number. Find another instance of that number, also in black. Which named location are you physically closest to?

8. Can you discover which English king and queen are associated with Ampthill?

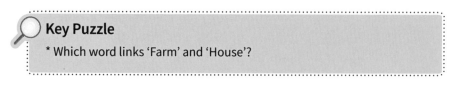

🔍 **Key Puzzle**
* Which word links 'Farm' and 'House'?

Map 28 BLETCHLEY PARK

'Before the Second World War, Bletchley Park was reasonably innocuous, in that very British way that so many places steeped in history can be said to be reasonably innocuous. Formerly owned by one of William the Conqueror's closest advisors, home to various mansions through history, and so on. But then Admiral Sinclair, the chief of the Secret Intelligence Service, purchased it out of his own pocket in 1938, because it was convenient for both Oxford and Cambridge, and he thought we'd likely need their help with the Nazis.'

I put on an innocent expression and asked Aunt Bea what the admiral had been like.

She arched an eyebrow at me, and continued as if I'd not interrupted. 'Bletchley – known variously as BP, Station X, London SigInt Centre and GCHQ – became the heart of the Allied cryptographic effort when war broke out. Our mathematical geniuses went to work here decrypting Axis communications, and they were incredibly successful. You will have heard of Alan Turing and quite rightly too. But did you know they also used the *Daily Telegraph* cryptic crossword to recruit?'

As usual, I had to admit that I did not.

'In 1942, they advertised for people to attend an event to test if the cryptic crossword was becoming too easy. Five of the attendees solved it under 12 minutes and a few weeks later they received an invitation to attendees Bletchley Park. You see, they knew that to solve this problem, they'd need people coming at it from every angle, lateral thinkers. Puzzle solvers.'

She winked at me.

'Anyway, it's no exaggeration to say that those teams of different sorts of brains shaved years off the war. Without them, it's entirely possible we'd have lost. Then, for a cherry on top, they created the world's first real modern computer, Colossus. The designer was called Tommy Flowers. Remember that next time you're poking at that phone of yours. Without Bletchley, the last 80 years would have been very different.'

QUESTIONS

Easy

1. Which canal is featured on the map?

2. Which location sounds like a ruddy heath?

Medium

3. During the Second World War, mathematicians and cryptanalysts working at Bletchley Park played a pivotal role in leading the Allies to victory. This was thanks in no small part to the decryption of a now-famous German cipher machine. What was it called?

4. How many different stations are indicated on the map?

Tricky

5. Multiply the numbers of the two A-roads printed on the map, then divide by the highest printed contour line value in western Bletchley. What number do you get, rounding down to the nearest hundred?

6. Which is the odd one out?
   a. FORD   b. LAND   c. MOOR   d. WEIR

Challenging

7. Can you find locations on the map that are anagrams of the following words or phrases? Ignore the spaces and punctuation, which may differ from those in the place names.
   a. A BLANK PROLOGUE   b. WHATNOT PIG
   c. TRENDY AFFRONTS   d. A TOWN-EATER

8. Can you decrypt the following simple cipher to discover the name of a famous code-breaker? GNIR UTNOS IHTA MNALA

Key Puzzle
   * Where is there an academy?

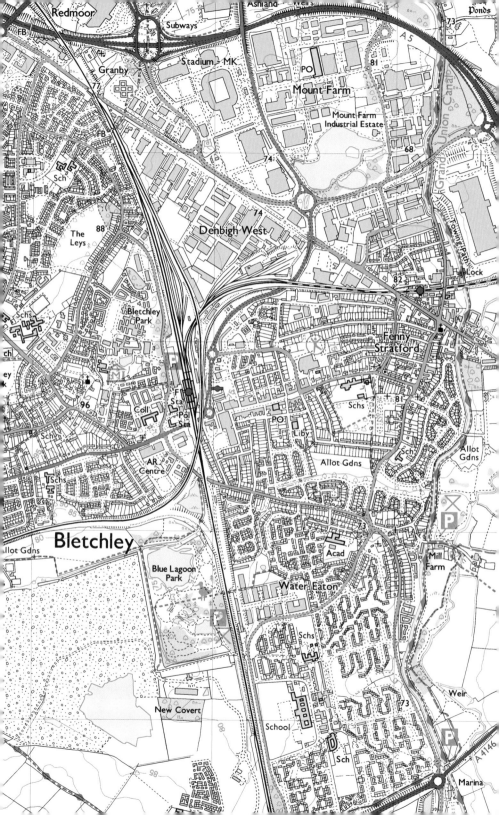

Map 29 WINDSOR CASTLE

'Normally I don't like people describing something as majestic, but with this place it's pretty much a statement of definition rather than a description.'

We were approaching Windsor Castle from the Long Walk, weaving in and out of the groups of tourists.

'It's been the seat of English royalty for almost a thousand years. William the Conqueror had it built to protect London from the rest of England, and prevent enemies from just sailing down the Thames, but since then it's become one of the most enduring symbols of our monarchy. Inside and out, it is spectacular but tasteful, imposing but accessible, ancient but modern.'

Around us, the Great Park spread away from the castle in three directions. I thought again about Aunt Bea's point about landscapes being the product of human activity, which felt particularly relevant here. Everything in the park has been carefully thought-out, shaped to fit the needs and preferences of kings and queens, one after the other, down through the centuries.

'Just under 20 monarchs have called this place home. Multiple Henrys, Georges and Edwards, a pair of Charleses, a Victoria and both Elizabeths. My favourite story is about King George VI and his wife Queen Elizabeth, who were living here when the Second World War broke out but who stayed in Buckingham Palace during the London bombardments because they felt they must stay with their subjects. That knot of duty between the monarch, the people and the country. I can't pretend to untie it, or say it's a simple one. There is a different gravity to this place than at Loch Ness or Ben Nevis but it is here. You feel it. The heart of the monarchy's power.'

Easy

1. How many libraries are indicated on the map?

2. Which monarch has an entrance listed by name?

Medium

3. How many different numbered roads are labelled on the map?

4. Which location on the map sounds as if it may be owned by one of the Twelve Apostles?

Tricky

5. Who was the first reigning monarch to use Windsor Castle as a home?

6. Find two nearby routes at different speeds. Where they meet, follow northwards. Examine the second animal you pass alongside. Which residence shares its name?

Challenging

7. According to legend, a mythological figure is said to have been associated with a specific tree located within the area covered by the map. Can you discover that figure's identity? Bear in mind that HE HURT RENE THEN.

8. Can you find locations on the map that are anagrams of the following words or phrases? Ignore the spaces and punctuation, which may differ from those in the place names.
   a. RAMMED LOGO   b. OUR MOUSEY LLAMA
   c. SORE BATCH   d. FLAME PARTICLE

Key Puzzle

* Which path is south of an old Park Pale?

Map 30 EPSOM RACE COURSE

'We've been racing horses almost since we first domesticated them 6,000 years ago. So it's a very human activity. We're a competitive lot, and it's just one of the many ways we've picked to test each other,' Aunt Bea told me.

'The resident of our previous stop, Queen Elizabeth herself, is a lover of horses, and is said to read the *Racing Post* over breakfast every morning. I'm sure she'd approve of us coming here next.'

There was no race to see but we were walking down to the 'Epsom Downs', the area that was free for people to come and watch the races.

'They've been racing horses here officially since 1661, although apparently a burial list from 1625 refers to a man who "in running the race, fell from his horse and brake his neck", so who knows how long before that they actually were.'

I was a little surprised how hilly it was, as I'd imagined horse races were flat affairs.

'Britain has very varied racecourses, each with its own particular set of challenges and trials. Of course, it is big business nowadays. You have to be well-heeled to own a thoroughbred, and the gambling it supports is enormous – tens of billions a year at the very least. So, while Epsom is a reigning pinnacle of a vast, fully modern industry, it is also the inheritor of an ancient tradition going back millennia.'

I imagined how many horses over the centuries had raced around this course. How many millions of people had stood and watched hopefully. Aunt Bea pointed into the distance.

'That there is Tattenham Corner, the final corner before the home straight. It was there on 4 June 1913 that the suffragette Emily Davison ducked under the guardrail and stood in front of Anmer, King George V's horse, trying to reach for the reins. She was struck by the horse and died four days later. The horses are huge when you're here and they come thundering around that corner. It means something else to see it for ourselves rather than to read it in a book, doesn't it?'

I nodded thoughtfully.

'Big fairs used to be held here to coincide with major race events. Sometimes, they even closed parliament so that the nation's politicians could come and take part in the fun. I see the doubt in your eyes, young man. However you may feel about horses, Epsom is a part of Britain's national identity, and it links us to traditions from the dawn of our civilisation.'

■ Easy

1. Which famous race is held on the first Saturday in June every year at Epsom Race Course?

2. Which place on the map might be the least hospitable?

■ Medium

3. How many place names on the map feature words generally associated with horses and horse racing?

4. What sport is the nearest available one to the clubhouse?

■ Tricky

5. Draw a straight line through four words that include the letters 'ley'. It passes through two unrelated names on the map. What are they?

6. What type of apparel is most celebrated on Epsom Race Course's famous Ladies' Day?

■ Challenging

7. Can you find locations on the map that are anagrams of the following words or phrases? Ignore the spaces and punctuation, which may differ from those in the place names.
    a. BANSHIE BLAME   b. OLD HEARSAY
    c. WITS-FUDDLING FRAME   d. THE TRANCE MATRON

8. Leaving the longest building just east of Twistwood, head north along a bridleway. Continue downhill until you reach the inhospitable place you found earlier. Take the number of metres you have descended and multiply it by the total number of public telephones and railway stations. Finally, subtract the largest B-road number. What number are you left with?

🔍 Key Puzzle

* What is denoted by the blue symbol east of a public house?

Map 31 GREENWICH

'Navigating the world in the eighteenth century had a large element of hit and miss about it. In order to work out where you were in the middle of the sea, you needed to know both your latitude – how far north or south you were – and your longitude – how far east or west you were. Latitude could be worked out relatively easily by working out the angle between the noon sun or a constellation and the ship and the visible horizon. When you put this angle into a nautical almanac, this gave you your degrees latitude – how far north or south of the equator you were. But longitude, how far east or west you were, was much trickier. There is no naturally occurring equivalent to the equator. There were various methods involving constellations and the moon but they were complicated, unwieldy and unreliable. The most precise was to use the angle of the sun, but for that you needed a fixed point, with a fixed time and a clock set to that time, so that you could work out how different the angle of the sun was to the fixed point at that time of day. And for many years it was thought impossible that any clock would ever be created that could keep time accurately while on a ship at sea. Because of the distances involved, even an error of a minute could mean that you were miles off course. That was until a remarkable self-taught clockmaker called John Harrison invented what became known as the H4 chronometer and ushered in a new era.'

We were stood looking down over the green hill and white buildings spread beneath us. At 180 acres, according to the information board,

Greenwich Park is one of the largest areas of natural land in south-east London. Well, 'natural' land anyway. There are some amazing views towards central and east London from its hills. You can even make out the Gherkin in the heart of the City. It's a pretty place, with lots of really beautiful old buildings around it.

'It's been a piece of enclosed parkland since 1433,' Aunt Bea said. 'It's been worked on, of course, particularly in the seventeenth century. Henry VIII introduced the deer, so he could hunt them, and various other alterations have been made. The Queen's House was built in the early 1600s, the Royal Observatory was finished in 1676 and the Greenwich Hospital arrived in 1705. They've all played their roles in shaping the park. Of all of them, it's the Observatory that really captures my imagination. What I wouldn't give to be able to explore the stars!'

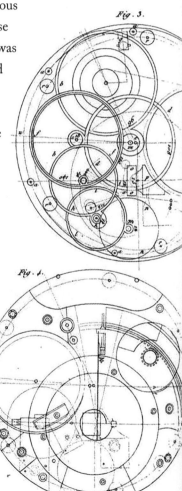

It was all too easy to imagine Aunt Bea wanting to drag me off into space and give me a tour of the local star systems. I counted myself lucky that it wasn't an option open to us.

'Of all the places we've been, the Royal Observatory at Greenwich is the one that has the deepest, strongest place in the British psyche. It's the G in GMT, and our day is defined by reference to this very place. Every time we look at a clock or a watch – and oh how ruled by time we all are – we're reinforcing its importance in our lives.'

QUESTIONS

Easy

1. What famously passes through the Royal Observatory?

2. Counting the top grid row of the map as 1, which row has the most train stations?

Medium

3. How many different A- and B-roads have their numbers shown on the map?

4. Apart from Britain itself, how many islands appear on the map, and where?

Tricky

5. What type of ship is the *Cutty Sark*? Bear in mind the PLATE PRICE.

6. At which location on the map are you likely to find the most officers of the law?

Challenging

7. Can you reassemble the following fragments to find four words printed on the map? ACK, BL, DGE, HE, HOL, IME, IT, LL, LY, MAR, OB, ORY, SER, VAT, WA

8. Can you discover for which queen a residence shown on the map was built?

Key Puzzle

* Which of the roads shown on the map has the lowest number?

Map 32 WHITE CLIFFS OF DOVER

'If you're waiting to see bluebirds over these cliffs, you'll be waiting a long time, my boy,' said Aunt Bea, striding off towards the cliffs from the car park. 'Bluebirds are an American species. Of course, it's been said that the bluebird in the song is a reference to the US Air Force. And so many people found solace in its message of hope for tomorrow during the Second World War, that it is perhaps best not to be too pedantic about these things.'

The sky was high and a pale blue as we walked up the hill, and it wasn't hard to imagine planes wheeling overhead. France felt very close on that coast.

'Anyway, if Greenwich is the internal mechanism of British self-identity, the spring that keeps it ticking over, then the White Cliffs of Dover are that identity's outer casing.'

I thought about that for a moment. We were near the top of the cliff, with the port of Dover tucked off down to the right, and the coast of France dimly visible 21 miles away.

'The White Cliffs are our national symbol of defiance, of resilience – the shining walls of our castle Britain, lovely and unsullied. If there was any

historic room for doubt about that, the evacuation of Dunkirk settled it. It's not true, of course. Britain has been invaded and occupied over and over again, Neolithic folk, Beaker People, Celts, Romans, Anglo-Saxons, Danes, Normans, a parade of peoples coming over and settling, falling in love with the land, becoming part of the tapestry that is Britain.'

I asked if that was unusual, compared to other nations.

'Of course not! We're a fractious species, particularly where territory is involved. Every scrap of land has been fought over time and again, lost and won and lost again. Nations are a group delusion, when you get down to it. But having said that, the land shapes us, and dear old Albion is a green and pleasant place. This is fertile soil for mystery and legend, and these great white cliffs are definitely an important part of that. A rock made from the compressed bodies of sea creatures who died 70 or so million years ago, now glowing from the edge of the country, given meaning by some primates who only gained the ability to speak 150,000 years ago. The blink of an eye really. We're getting closer to our destination, our prize. You can feel it, can't you?'

She was right. I could.

■ Easy

1. What is the location that sounds like a source of food located a short way south of a source of hunger?

2. How many masts are shown on the map?

■ Medium

3. Which material gives the White Cliffs their colour?

4. Which of these words is the odd one out?
   a. WALL   b. TREE
   c. RIOT   d. SHIP

■ Tricky

5. How many different locations on the map include the letters required to spell the word 'beer'?

6. Add the values of the different A-road numbers shown on the map, then subtract the highest orange number shown. Add twice the number of letters in the name of the hungriest place on the map, and find a contour line marked with that height. Which hotel does it pass through?

■ Challenging

7. Assuming an average speed of a mile every 50 minutes, how long would it take to swim the Channel and back?

8. Can you reassemble the following fragments to find four words printed on the map? ADL, ARY, BRI, BRO, CH, CK, EES, ELD, ERR, FI, LIT, MI, REE, YT

Key Puzzle
* What is the name of the rhombic patch of scrubland and non-coniferous trees?

Map 33 POOH STICKS BRIDGE

According to Aunt Bea, people have been living in Ashdown Forest for 50,000 years.

It's not particularly wooded, for a forest – most of it is open heath, which rolls gently over the downs.

'That's a very human effect. Left alone, heath in these parts becomes woodland fairly quickly,' Aunt Bea told me.

'Ashdown's wood and grazing land were important resources for centuries, so the trees were kept down. The woodland rebounded after the Second World War, and now a trust keeps the balance manually. There's evidence of Bronze Age, Iron Age and Roman settlements in the locality. The forest as we see it now has its origins in a hunting forest the Normans created shortly after the invasion and over the centuries many monarchs came here to get their deer fix, including Henry VIII. However, the animals it's probably most famous for now are a bear, a piglet, a donkey, a rabbit and a tiger. And innumerable heffalumps of course.'

I stopped walking and looked at her with my eyebrows raised.

'A. A. Milne's Hundred Acre Wood was based on a chunk of true woodland that had been in private hands since the seventeenth century, preserved rather than exploited. Anyone who's read a Winnie-the-Pooh book knows how lovely it is.' She paused. 'You have read Winnie-the-Pooh, haven't you?'

I assured her that I had.

'I should really have packed us some honey sandwiches of course, as there are a couple of spots you'll recognise from the stories. And I'm afraid you and I will certainly have to face trial by stick combat. It has always seemed so quintessentially British that pooh sticks has become not only a real sport, but an internationally contested one at that. Delight in gentle whimsy is, I believe, one of our most important features, the cornerstone of our famous humour and eccentricity. It's one of our best characteristics, my boy, and I urge you to pursue it wherever possible.'

I told her that this entire treasure hunt appeared to fit that description, and she beamed broadly at me.

'My dear boy, if you take nothing else away from our trip, I hope it is that there are very few places that do not yield treasure with a small amount of investigation. The stations on our journey have taken us to places of great fascination. Yet at every stage, we have been surrounded by an enormous array of alternatives. And finally, that little bear has perhaps the greatest description of navigating ever put to paper. "I am not lost, for I know where I am. But however, where I am may be lost."'

▨ Easy

1. Going by its name, what is the gate said to be made of?

2. What might be the strangest place on the map?

▨ Medium

3. Can you pair up the following words to make four words printed on the map? COTCH, DING, FORD, HURST, KILN, SHAW, STAN, WOOD

4. How many farms are shown on the map?

▨ Tricky

5. Find the most comfortable hill on which to lay your head. What is the air survey height number directly south of it?

6. Can you find out the supposed size of the patch of woodland that was the real basis of Hundred Acre Wood?

▨ Challenging

7. Which locations sound like a home for the following:
   a. a single tree
   b. a dark protuberance
   c. a place for sweaters
   d. an avian maze
   e. the stem of a vegetable

8. From a triangulation pillar, follow a path south to a B-road. Nearby is a junction with a minor road. If you travel the minor road from that junction to a ford, how many contour lines do you pass through?

🔍 Key Puzzle

* Where, per the map, can you take riding lessons?

Map 34 HEVER CASTLE

'So after a hard day's hunting in Ashdown Forest, Henry VIII would likely have returned here. What a place to come home to. And, of course, as things transpired it would play a key role in the violent birth of a new England.'

Aunt Bea was gesturing up at Hever Castle and she was right, it was truly lovely. It's not a military emplacement like Caernarfon Castle, though it's on the site of a medieval defensive castle, nor does it have the same sort of display of power as somewhere like Windsor Castle. Instead, it feels like a fairy-tale castle.

That's not to say it looks undefended – the walls are strong and battlemented, and there's a moat and drawbridge – but everything is designed with an eye to aesthetic taste as well. It's a home, and a beautiful one at that.

The grounds reflect this as well. There are rose gardens, Italianate courtyards, a charming ornamental lake, carefully sculpted topiary displays, herb beds, pretty cottages, a glasshouse full of ferns and even a couple of mazes. These features aren't all ancient – the earliest of the mazes, a yew maze, is only 115 or so years old – but it's extremely easy to become lost in the sense of medieval beauty that the castle and grounds exude. Our visit didn't coincide with one of the medieval jousting or archery tournaments unfortunately. That would have been fun to watch.

While Aunt Bea was consulting our maps and notebook, and muttering quietly to herself about intrigue and Henry VIII, I was mostly enjoying the scenery. We still found our solution and the lead to our next step, but I do admit that I was less help than usual.

Easy

1. What is the area of the named island?

2. How many public houses are indicated on the map?

Medium

3. Which two place names might suggest animals have been lowered?

4. Can you pair up these words to make four names that appear in locations on the map? BRIDGE, BROOK, ELMS, GREEN, HOUSE, LAND, NEW, POLE

Tricky

5. What sounds like the most remote location on the map?

6. Which of Henry VIII's wives spent much of her young life at Hever Castle?

Challenging

7. Find a hole in a rail tunnel and follow the contour line that passes through it to the nearest farm as the raven flies. Head north to a place that sounds like a pub, then eastwards to the nearest road. From that point, travel directly north until you reach a name. Where are you?

8. Newtye Hurst is a location towards the south edge of the map. What, in this instance, is a hurst?

Key Puzzle

 * Where might you look for an orchard?

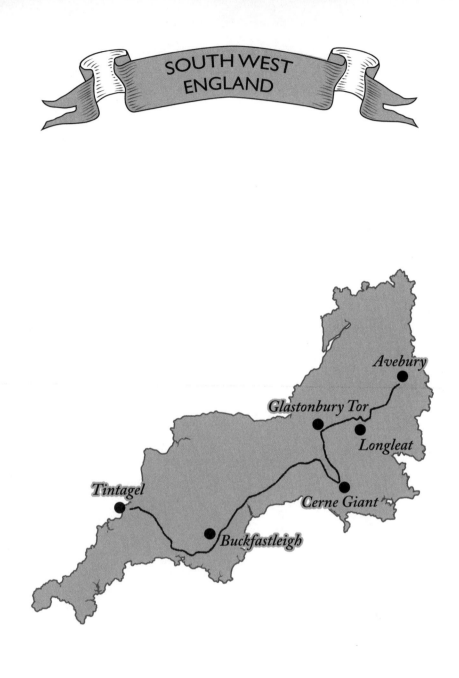

SOUTH WEST
ENGLAND

Avebury

Glastonbury Tor

Longleat

Tintagel

Cerne Giant

Buckfastleigh

NORTH SEA

ENGLISH
CHANNEL

Map 35 AVEBURY

'Stonehenge might be more spectacular, with its towering trilithons and hundreds of tumuli, and it richly deserves its fame, but Avebury is the largest Neolithic stone circle in the world,' Aunt Bea declared. 'And it's only one of a great many sites in this area from the Neolithic and Bronze Ages. There's Silbury Hill, The Sanctuary and West Kennet Long Barrow, The Avenue and a host of less celebrated but equally fascinating places. We are standing in a vast sacred landscape, about which we know very little. We think there were feasts, large gatherings of people but who knows why. So much of the past has been lost to us but the clues are everywhere if you know how to look.'

It certainly seemed like that where we were, standing inside the circle's south-west sector, just off the village high street. It's an eerie experience, seeing a village built inside a stone circle. Sure, most of the stones have gone over the years, but enough of them remain to make the buildings feel haunted by the deep past. Besides, the surrounding earthworks would be perfectly capable of dominating the local environment all on their own.

'Unfortunately, the stones became associated with the Devil during the eleventh or twelfth century. The site suffered badly as a result – many stones were broken up for building material, and others were toppled and buried. Legend has it that during the toppling of one stone, a man was crushed to death, and the people were unable to retrieve his body for a proper burial. After that, the remaining stones were left alone, to prevent further retaliation. The body of a fourteenth-century barber-surgeon was found beneath one of the buried stones in 1938, in fact, but there was no sign of death by crushing, so who knows. Just one of the many mysteries and puzzles clustered here.' She tapped the notebook meaningfully. It was time to get to work.

QUESTIONS

Easy

1. What is the height of the triangulation pillar?
2. Which bridge shares its name with a Greek deity?

Medium

3. Which amenities can you find within Avebury stone circle?
4. What is unusual about Silbury Hill?

Tricky

5. Where on the map can you find a wind pump?
6. Which location sounds like an area where deer gather to mate?

Challenging

7. Take the number of times the words Tumuli or Tumulus appear on the map, and add this to the lowest air or ground survey height adjacent to a car park. What number do you end up with?
8. Starting on a mound, head north to an aerially surveyed height mark. Find another such point four metres higher. A short way to the north-east, a black line leads off. Follow it to near a pair of tumuli. From the more northerly of the pair, strike directly westwards. What is the first pair of words associated with a single location that you pass between?

Key Puzzle

* What does the tourist and leisure symbol that appears precisely three times on the map indicate that you may do?

Map 36 LONGLEAT

'The house is a fine example of Elizabethan architecture set in a thousand acres of Capability Brown landscaping, and the interiors are most impressive, but it was inheritance tax that turned Longleat into what it is today.'

We were inside the extensive hedge maze, and we'd gotten a little turned around. I gently suggested to Aunt Bea that she was stalling and that perhaps, like Pooh, we knew where we were, but where we were might have become lost.

'Not at all,' she protested, as we turned back from another dead end. 'Longleat has been groundbreaking in so many ways, and it's all because financial trouble forced the issue. The original house was built on the site of an old priory that had burned down in the mid-sixteenth century and it is commonly agreed to be one of the finest pieces of Elizabethan architecture in the whole country. It stayed in the Thynne family for the next 13 generations. But when Henry Frederick Thynne inherited it in 1946, it came with a huge debt. So he decided to try to make the house pay its own way. Of course, his peers at the time were horrified. It was thought preferable by some even to let the house be demolished, rather than sully it with the grubby whiff of commerce. But it was a tremendous success and others quickly followed suit. Longleat in the modern era has a history of firsts. When it opened in 1966, it was the first safari park in existence outside Africa, for example. That was the brainchild of Jimmy Chipperfield of Chipperfield's Circus fame. Once the park was established, anyone could come and see exotic animals from other continents in the countryside, rather than in cages or being poked around a ring. Giraffes, monkeys, tigers, lions, wolves, rhinos, cheetahs – there are all

sorts of popular creatures here. The miniature railway is one of the busiest in the country, and runs for more than a mile. Or take this maze, even. It's one of the longest yew hedge mazes in the world, and it's just one of five that the seventh Marquess of Bath designed for the grounds.'

I pointed out that this bit of the maze felt very familiar.

'I think that was an "island wall".' She reached out and touched the other side of the maze with her hand.

'Now it's simply a case of touching this wall and walking until we get out of the maze. Not the most efficient way to solve it, but as long as we keep our hand always touching the same side, it is the most reliable. While we're walking, you can talk me through the next lot of clues. Perhaps we can exercise our brains as well as our legs.'

QUESTIONS

■ Easy

1. Which country is named on the map?

2. Which predators are most strongly associated with Longleat Safari Park?

■ Medium

3. Which named location is directly east of the symbol used on the map to indicate Longleat House?

4. How many ponds and pools are named on the map?

■ Tricky

5. Can you find locations on the map that could mean the following:
   a. milk wood   b. entrance to paradise
   c. chunk of igloo   d. extended row of bushes

6. In 1949, Longleat House became the first British stately home to do what?

■ Challenging

7. Can you pair the following words together to form seven words printed on the map? BURY, CARP, COMBE, ENTER, HEDGE, HIT, HOUSE, LAND, LONG, NEW, POOL, RAG, RUSH, WOOD

8. Moving directly from the highest point of Park Hill to the bottom-left of an 'other tourist feature' symbol, you will pass through more than one contour line height value. Find the mean average of these numbers, and divide this by the sum of the number of times the words 'Wood' and 'Coppice' appear on the map. Multiply the result by 10, and find this number written on the map in orange. If you follow this contour line northwards, what is the first named location you come to?

○ Key Puzzle

* Which location is a short distance east of a viewpoint?

Map 37 GLASTONBURY TOR

Standing on the top of Glastonbury Tor on a clear day gives you the feeling that half of south-western England is spread out before you. A fine reward for our hour and a bit's walk. It's not that much of a lie, either. The Tor rises up 500 feet out of the wide plains of Somerset, and it's been an important landmark for centuries. Its slopes are carved into seven symmetrical terraces that have been dated back to the Neolithic period, but no one really knows why.

'The terraces are just a fraction of it,' Aunt Bea told me when I asked. 'Glastonbury Tor attracts legends and mystery like a magnet attracts iron. One persistent myth is that after arranging for Christ's burial after the Crucifixion, Joseph of Arimathea came to Glastonbury Tor by boat. Some people have suggested that he was Christ's great-uncle on his mother's side, which I like! Anyhow, Joseph's purpose in coming to the damp, misty edge of the known world was to secure safekeeping for the Holy Grail. This was the cup that Jesus had used at the Last Supper, and which Joseph had then used to catch his blood during the Crucifixion. When he landed on Albion,

CHEDDAR GOR
MENDIP HILLS
Wells & Glastonbury

OS EXPLORER
1:25 000 scale   4 cm to 1 km - 2½ inches to 1 mile

here at the Tor, he placed his walking staff upright in the ground and took a much-needed nap. He awoke to discover that the staff had regained its life to become a hawthorn three, complete with roots and bloom-covered branches. I could go on for hours, about the twice-blooming Glastonbury Thorn, or the Zodiac, or the Chalice Well, or the coffins, or even the odd idea that the Grail was actually a child of Christ's. Glastonbury has claim to being one of the hearts of pagan and Christian Britain. Of course, to most people, the word Glastonbury is inextricably linked to the music festival that first began as a party in a field in 1970. These days around 200,000 people come to commune with music and revelry. I'd like to think they are continuing the great traditions of shared spiritual experience here.'

I squinted at Aunt Bea, trying to imagine her jumping up and down in a field.

'So is that based on personal experience, Aunt Bea?'

'That's one puzzle you'll have to solve yourself, my dear boy.'

QUESTIONS

■ Easy

1. What is on top of Glastonbury Tor?

2. Which mythic king is strongly associated with Glastonbury?

■ Medium

3. What word for an open ditch or drainage channel appears in four different names on the map?

4. Which sounds like the most tiring place on the map? And how about a place for driving cattle across water?

■ Tricky

5. Multiply the number of boundary stones indicated on the map by the number of footbridges. Find a location of that survey height, and head north to an A-road. Turn right along that road and, sticking to routes navigable by car, take the next two lefts and then the first right. Proceed to a larger road. What is on the other side of that road?

6. What now well-known name did the ancient Britons use for Glastonbury Tor?

■ Challenging

7. Can you find locations on the map that are anagrams of the following words or phrases? Ignore the spaces and punctuation, which may differ from those in the place names.
   a. FAIRER GLEN   b. DREARY HEADMEN
   c. CRABLIKE TV POD   d. DRIFTING AMBER

8. Can you discover the fate of Glastonbury's last abbot?

Key Puzzle

* Subtract one less than the number of farms named on the map from the number of the road that runs north of a factory. What do you get?

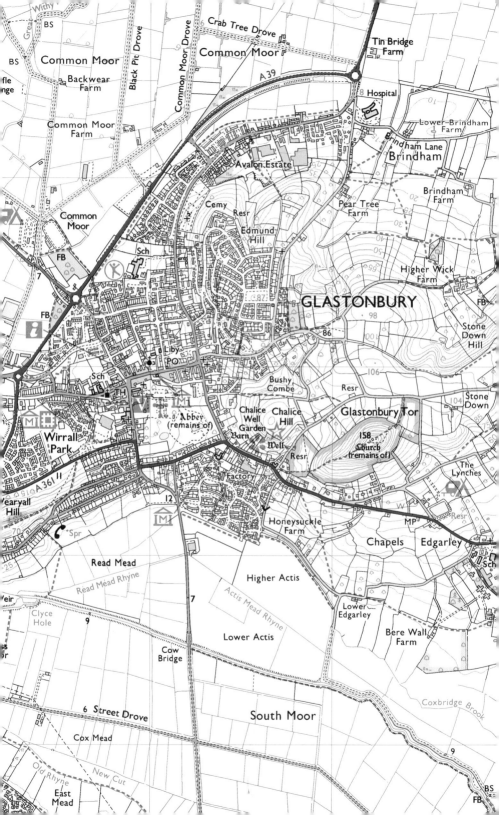

Map 38 CERNE GIANT

The Giant of Cerne Abbas is, well, odd. Eccentric, even. It's a chalk pictogram, cut out of the grass on the slope of a hill overlooking the village, and it depicts a tall, naked and significantly aroused man wielding a large, irregularly shaped club in one hand. The other hand is outstretched, and perhaps waving in greeting.

'It is a fact that anyone who has seen the schoolbooks of children knows only too well. Give someone a blank canvas and, at some point, someone is going to draw one of those on it,' laughed Aunt Bea in the car park.

'We'll walk up closer to it in a while, but the best view is actually from down here. People used to assume that the Giant was prehistoric, 3,000 or more years old like the White Horse of Uffington. Folklorists assumed it was a depiction of Hercules, or perhaps some early deity whose name has slipped into the mists. And to be fair to them, it could be the case. The thing is that we don't have any mention of it dated before 1694, and there are land survey reports from 1617 that don't allude to it at all. That's not definitive proof, of course, but it's certainly indicative. He used to have a cloak draped over his free arm, which could strengthen the idea of Hercules with the pelt of the Nemean Lion. Oliver Cromwell was occasionally known as England's

Hercules, so there's one theory that it's basically a gigantic middle finger at him – one of his bitter enemies, Lord Holles, owned the land at the time. I think I might even prefer that idea to it being some very earnest act of Celtic devotion two millennia ago. Feels more British as an act of offensive defiance, somehow. And, of course, reminds us that the land around us is always in conversation with the mores of the time. What begins as a joke becomes an object of serious study. Entire edifices of knowledge are tipped upon their head by one finding that challenges it all. History is a living thing, changing as our understanding changes, and we are surrounded by it everywhere we go on this island. Anyway, let's take our next lot of clues up to the giant. I very much hope that "X" doesn't mark one particular spot.'

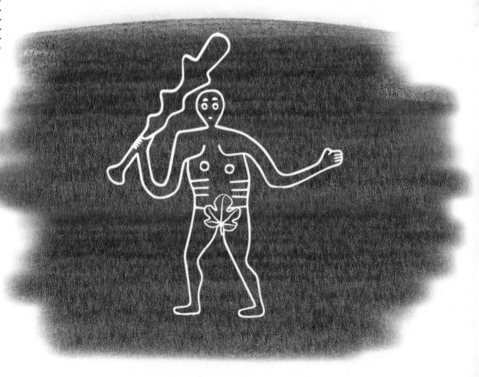

QUESTIONS

■ Easy

1. Outside of the map square that contains the Cerne Abbas Giant, which location name refers to a body part of the chalk figure?

2. How many Bottoms are there on the map?

■ Medium

3. How many tumuli are shown on the map?

4. What adjective is missing here from the Cerne Abbas Giant's informal nickname, The ____ Man of Cerne? He is a hearty, abrupt, roughly made and uneducated fellow.

■ Tricky

5. Which of these is the odd one out?
   a. Black   b. Bow's
   c. Dickley   d. Rowden

6. If you travel due south towards the coast from Cerne Abbas, which lighthouse, whose name is inspired by a bird appendage, do you reach? It's an ALL BLOND TRIP.

■ Challenging

7. Can you discover the date of the earliest known written reference to the Giant?

8. From the highest marked spot on the map, head to the nearest footpath that does not permit horses. Follow that to a place where it diverges. A word is printed there. Directly to the south, the same word is again printed. From the final letter of that repeated word, head north to the first contour line, and follow it until it crosses the name of a wood. What is the next named location to the north?

🔍 Key Puzzle

* Which elevated area includes an aerial survey height of 213m?

Map 39 BUCKFASTLEIGH

'It feels only right that we enter the home straight of our adventure here. In the footsteps of one of the greatest fictional clue solvers there has ever been. Do you know *The Hound of the Baskervilles*?'

I assured Aunt Bea that even I had heard of that one.

'Well, Brook Manor was the home of a fellow called Richard Cabell in the seventeenth century, the squire of Buckfastleigh, and he was a notorious evil-doer who was obsessed with hunting. All sorts of rumours surrounded him, including that he had called up the Devil and sold his soul, and that after hearing suggestions of infidelity, he forced his wife out onto the moors and then hunted her down, stabbing her to death when he'd tired of the chase. When he finally died, hellhounds appeared all over the moors and raced around howling and breathing fire, eventually surrounding the Manor. Cabell was buried in the churchyard, but on the anniversary of his death, he and his hellhounds would rise again and hunt on the moors. Sometimes he'd be in a carriage drawn by a headless horse – which makes a change from a headless horseman.'

'I'd prefer neither!'

'When Conan Doyle came to write the third of his Sherlock Holmes books, it is believed to be this legend he leaned on for the Baskervilles. A fascinating fellow, Arthur Conan Doyle. The creator of one of the most famous rational empiricists the world has ever known, and yet he was a massive believer in ghosts and seances. In fact, six days after his death in 1930, a mass seance was held at the Royal Albert Hall, so that he might have the opportunity to communicate from beyond the grave.'

'And?'

Dartmsor

'No luck, of course. Anyway, it's further said that in order to keep the dastardly squire in his proper place, the villagers of Buckfastleigh covered his grave with a heavy stone slab, and constructed a small prison-like sepulchre around it. Despite this, people have reported seeing a hellish red glow oozing out through the bars, and some have even mentioned seeing hellhounds and other demons clustered around the sepulchre, attempting to free the squire. Historical records contradict most of this, of course, but in a cave directly below the sepulchre, there really is a strange figure in the shape of a man, possibly winged, that was apparently formed naturally by a stalactite and stalagmite meeting.'

■ Easy

1. How many boundary stones are shown on the map?

2. Which location on the map might you see in the sky?

■ Medium

3. There is a 'south' on the map further north than a 'north'. What type of location are they?

4. The Sherlock Holmes novel *The Hound of the Baskervilles*, inspired by a legend linked to Brook Manor, takes place mostly on which sharp moor?

■ Tricky

5. Can you pair together the following pieces to make four words appearing on the map? BLACK, CAMP, FORD, GLEBE, HANNA, HILL, LANDS, MOOR

6. Which places on the map sound like the following:

   a. a happy meadow
   c. something useful for a tailor

   b. an angry man
   d. a blessed stream

■ Challenging

7. Can you discover the nickname of the evil squire whose legendary death inspired Sir Arthur Conan Doyle's *The Hound of the Baskervilles*?

8. Add the two highest numbers on the map in black to the number of places described as a ruin. Divide by 10, and find the resulting number on the map, then to that add the orange numbers to the west that are within the same grid row. Take that number, add 2, and then divide by 10. Rearrange the resulting digits to match an orange number on the map. Which location is the first you come to from there, moving east?

○ Key Puzzle

* What is the title of the person to whom a wood on the map supposedly belongs?

⳼Map 40 TINTAGEL

'This is the final place on our trail, my boy. The last breadcrumb, or at least the last one I've been able to find any clear references to in my notes. I'm hoping that what we learn here, with everything else we have discovered, will open the lock of this treasure chest we've been exploring.'

Aunt Bea and I were sat on a bench, looking down over the headland at the Cornish sea.

I nodded, feeling suddenly a little glum at the prospect it was nearly over.

'Let's take a moment to appreciate how far we've come. From the far north-west of these islands, down to the far south-west. We've passed through thousands of years of human history, millions of years of Earth's history. And, I think, you may even have enjoyed some of it.'

I smiled. It was true. Whatever this led to, I'd had an amazing time journeying round Britain's wonders with Aunt Bea. I had expected to be desperate to get home to my normal life by now, but . . . I wasn't. I was having far too much fun.

'What better place to end up than here at Tintagel, so bound to the legend of Arthur. There was no tactical value to this setting in the thirteenth century, but Richard, Earl of Cornwall, built a castle here because it was said to be the place where King Arthur was conceived. And, as we've seen, for him to have been present at every landmark that claims his presence, he would have to have been a very busy traveller.'

She patted me on the shoulder. 'Don't worry, lad. Britain is full of surprises and mysteries. There's one round every corner and another under every stone,

and you know to keep an eye out for them now. Besides, this is Tintagel Castle. Arthur's myth begins here in several important ways. Geoffrey of Monmouth claimed its association with Uther, Arthur and Merlin, but there's archaeological evidence too. The castle you can see is from the thirteenth century, but the site here truly does seem to have been occupied after the Romans abandoned Britain. Arthur's time. What's more, it appears to have been the site of a fort or palace used by regional royalty as a court and trade hub. King Arthur's Footprint might not be as misnamed as people assume.'

That was an intriguing possibility.

'Good man,' Aunt Bea said. 'Come now. The game's afoot, and we still don't know what we'll find at the end of the trail.'

▨ Easy

1. How many caves are listed on the map?

2. Which location seems particularly suitable for siblings?

▨ Medium

3. According to legend, which of Arthur's relatives lived at Tintagel Castle?

4. Can you find a place name that could mean 'further along the line'?

▨ Tricky

5. Which cliff is one letter away from sharing its name with a waterbird?

6. What do 'ale', 'bar', 'eat' and 'lick' all have in common?

▨ Challenging

7. From a farm where four rights of way meet, follow a road to a place that is 167m above sea level. Head directly west until you hit the sea, then south along the coast to a point. What other coastal feature shares the same name?

8. 'By Tre, Pol and Pen shall ye know all'... what?

🔍 Lock Puzzle

* 1-1 2-2 5-4 11-4 7-5 6-3 9-2 10-4 12-5 8-5 13-3 27-1 14-3 17-6 18-2 20-2 29-1 36-1 38-6 24-1 19-3 16-3 33-5 34-13 35-1 32-2 28-1 39-2 25-5

THE END OF AN ADVENTURE

Aunt Bea and I sat looking down over the sea as the sun set.

'That's it then?'

The final page of our book seemed to be nothing more than an impenetrable string of numbers. How was that supposed to tell us anything? All that way for nothing. But then I saw Aunt Bea's eyes light up.

'That's it! The whole time. It's a code telling us where to find the treasure. We'll need to go back through all of our papers and think laterally, but we're holding the answer in our hands, I know it!'

I hurriedly opened the book at the first page and began to flick back through our scrawled answers.

'Not yet, my dear boy.' She pointed towards the sea as it was stained with fire. 'Let's just enjoy this treasure for now.'

I reached for my phone to take a photograph, and realised I didn't know where I had packed it – but I didn't mind. We sat and listened to the sea against the rocks until the sun dipped behind the horizon.

'Right,' said Aunt Bea. 'Onwards.'

Now it's time to solve the treasure hunt.

Please visit **ospuzzlebook.co.uk** and enter your answer to the Lock Puzzle for the chance to win real treasure.

NORTH SEA

ENGLISH
CHANNEL

MAP

I

1. 854 (858 − 4. 858 from A858 near top left, 4 from the ground survey height on the same road, north-west of Cnoc na Cachalaidh)

2. 7 (Sheep Wash x 4 [1 east of Sgeir Shàldair, 1 north of Loch na Beinne Bige, 1 west of Tòb na Faodhail and 1 west of Linshader], Cattle Grid x 2 [1 north of Loch na Beinne Bige and 1 east of Tòb nan Leobag], and Sheep Dip x 1 [east of Gleann Culabhig])

3. The northerly one is further

4. 25 (there is a another one, but it is not between the school and the telephone)

5. The (Outer) Hebrides

6. The 5th row, with 3 wells

7. Sgeir an Eoin (Piers south of Rubha Arspaig, south to Linshader, round to jetty and across to contour south-east of Cnoc Buaile'n Da Ruisg, and up to school near Millhouse, then west to coast)

8. 13 (BAKER'S DOZEN)

Key Answer

* Island

MAP
2

1. Parking, a picnic site, a panoramic viewpoint and a recreation, leisure or sports centre

2. Coolin View

3. 1

4. Bonnie Prince Charlie

5. The (Inner) Hebrides

6. The mainland, by 35m (105 on Skye, just above Ceann Caol Druim a' Bhìdh, and 140 on the mainland, just above the waterfall)

7. Caisteal, Drochaid, Garnmore and Sgillinne

8. 1 (24 − 3 = 21 ÷ (3 + 4) = 3.3 is 1 less than 4)

> **Key Answer**
>
> * Loch na Bèiste ('Lake of the Beast')

MAP
3

1. Loch Bran

2. There are 5 Creags (Creag a' Ghiubhais, Creag Nighean Iain Duinn, Creag nam Broc, Creag Bhreac and Creag a' Chait) and 3 Carns (Carn Dubh, Carn a Bhreabadair and Carn na Dala-riach)

3. 150m

4. It is the largest by volume

5. 70m^3 (56km^2 = 56000000m^2. 1mm = 0.001m / 800 = 0.00000125. 560000000m^2 × 0.00000125m = 70m^3)

6. 228 (248 − 20. 248 at Creag Nighean Iain Duinn, 20 south of Foyers Bay)

7. They all appear within the names of Creags (Creag nam Broc, Creag a' Ghiubhais, Creag Nighean Iain Duinn and Creag a' Chait)

8. Aleister Crowley (he owned Boleskine House for 14 years, from 1899 to 1913)

> **Key Answer**
> * 1345 (134 × 10 = 1340 + 5)

MAP

4

1. The British Isles (therefore also of Great Britain, and of Scotland)

2. 3

3. 100 (South of the river, below the footbridge south of Màm Beag)

4. The observatory (The observatory is at 1340m, the castle is around 1100m and the Uamh Shomhairle cave is at 150m, so the observatory is 240m higher than the castle and 1190m higher than the cave)

5. A sharp ridge of rock

6. B4 (a 120m line goes through the bottom of 'Water' in the bottom right, and a 900m line very marginally just passes through the top left corner, giving a difference of 780m)

7. A wind turbine (72 in bottom left, to conifer symbol north of Alit an t-Snaig, north to U of Uamh Shomhairle, then north to CIC Hut)

8. Charles Thomson Rees Wilson

Key Answer

* 83 (135 + 31 = 166 ÷ 2)

MAP
5

1. Golf

2. Moon

3. 8 (1 unnamed hotel in Inveraray, 1 unnamed hotel in Newtown; 4 unnamed cairns north of Inveraray Golf Club)

4. Western (it is in Argyll & Bute)

5. Electric Cottage

6. Fish Farm, Salmon Leaps (or Salmon Draught Cottage), Malt Land and Cherrypark

7. a. Allt Riabhachan
   b. Standing Stone
   c. Creagh Dubh
   d. Brackley Wood

8. The nineteenth century; it opened in 1820

Key Answer

* Plantation (Tom-breac Plantation)

MAP
6

1. Ibrox Stadium (Rangers FC)

2. A theatre

3. The third, containing 17

4. Kelvinhaugh (it is the only labelled hospital complex)

5. They all appear in the map in pink (Kelvin*bridge*, K*inning* Park, Cess*nock* and *West* St)

6. The River Kelvin

7. *Christ of Saint John of the Cross*

8. The Botanic Gardens (11 in Ibrox, to Academy near south edge, to motorway, to Charing Cross Station, north to NTS site, west to A814 across the River Kelvin, north to B-road, and follow B-road to A82 intersection)

Key Answer
* Ferry

MAP
7

1. 7

2. Gallow Bank

3. Whinny Hill

4. Queensferry Crossing has the greatest length above water out of the three bridges

5. d. 'Maggie' is not printed anywhere on the map

6. 3m, south of the pier at West Ness

7. 71m (Cult Ness, to Town Pier, to Ferry Loch, to Ferry Hills)

8. Dunfermline

Key Answer
   * Harbour

MAP
8

1. 19m, at the remains of the Benedictine Priory

2. 2 (Bridge Well and Popple Well)

3. The Northumberland coast in the north-east of England

4. 3 (Bible Law, Black Law and Law Scap)

5. 44 (Guile Point to Oyster Scap, to The Basin, follow St Cuthbert's Way north where it breaks eastwards at 9, then onwards past 13, 7, 7 and 8 to Red Brae)

6. The Water Tower

7. a. Sheldrake Pool
   b. Bridge Well
   c. Riding Stone
   d. The Hainings

8. A facsimile of the Lindisfarne Gospels was gifted to the island in 1971, by Professor Suzanne Kaufman (The total of 1+9+7+1 = 18)

Key Answer
* Lough

MAP
9

1. 3 (Turret 37A, Turret 36A and Turret 35B)

2. Hadrian (as part of his fortified wall)

3. Hotbank Crags, Jenkins Burn and Knag Burn

4. Kennel Crags

5. 15 (Jingling Well, 1 east of Kingscrag Gate, 1 south of Bield, 1 east of Cragend, 1 north and 1 south-east of Broomlee Lough, 1 east of King's Wicket, 1 south of Housesteads, 1 east of New Beggarbog, 1 east and 2 south-west of Bradley, 1 west of West Crindledykes, 2 south of Bradleyhall Wood)

6. The Pennine Way, at 268 miles (Hadrian's Wall Path is 84 miles long; A Pennine Journey is not an official national trail, and is 247 miles long)

7. The River Esk (river-esque)

8. Beggarbog, Cultivation, Housesteads and Stangate

Key Answer

* Nature reserve

MAP

10

1. Cloven Barth

2. 141m

3. Hannah Moor

4. Poultry Farm, Eaglesfield and Peckmill

5. Waterbirds

6. 100m

7. a. Cloven Barth
   b. Rottington Hall
   c. Poultry Farm
   d. Scalebarrow

8. St Bees is a corruption of St Bega, an early medieval Irish princess who fled a pagan husband and was canonised

Key Answer

* Townhead

MAP

11

1. 4 (1 east of Ambleside, 1 north of Todd Crag and 2 south-east of Strawberry Wood)

2. You can catch a ferry

3. 5286, the number of the B-road into Clappersgate (though the greatest contour line height fully on the map is 300, east of Strawberry Wood)

4. Stencher Beck

5. 3 (5075 + 593 − 5286 = 382 ÷ 2 = 191 + 4 [Brathay Farm, Brathay Hall, Brathay Rocks and Brathay Garths] = 195 ÷ 3 = 65, 65m point on B5286 near Beck Pane Wood)

6. A mountain lake, specifically one hollowed out by glacial erosion

7. Tommy Brock, the badger (Brock Crag and Brockhole)

8. d. Gale (it is the only one not written on a green background anywhere on the map)

$\bigcirc$ **Key Answer**
* Vicarage

MAP

12

1. Count Dracula

2. Shawn Riggs

3. Golden Grove

4. St Bennedict. (Whitby Abbey was a Bennedictine Abbey)

5. a. Castle (the others all appear within the names of farms on the map)

6. 5 (A174, B1416, B1460, A171 and B1410)

7. As of 2020, the ceremony of the Penny Hedge was 861 years old

8. 51m (The Scar, to Airy Hill Farm, to the cemetery church, to the peak above Spital Vale)

Key Answer

* West Cliff

MAP

13

1. The twentieth century

2. Hesslewood Hall

3. Gravel Pit Road

4. E2

5. 5 (4 birds [nature reserves] and 1 fish [fishing])

6. Lincolnshire and East Riding of Yorkshire (EAST YORKSHIRE and NORTH LINCOLNSHIRE to be precise)

7. a. Ness
   b. Viking
   c. Whelps
   d. Haven
   e. Ings

8. M, in black (15 buildings. Number is on south end of A15. 10m contour line to unnamed rise west of Gravel Pit Road. Straight north takes you through the M of 'Motel' and the A15/A63 roundabout)

Key Answer

* Plantation

MAP

14

1. Little John

2. 94m (west of Centre Tree)

3. *Ceres* Lodge and *Halfmoon* Plantation

4. Prehistoric (the forest has been scientifically dated at around 12,000 years old)

5. Hanger Hill Wood (Blackpool Plantation to triangular patch of woodland near 93m peak, to track across bottom of larger forest area and follow directions along Robin Hood Way to Centre Tree, north past Sunnyside Wood, to Hanger Hill Wood)

6. The twelfth century (during the absentee rule of King Richard I)

7. a. Centre Tree
   b. Seymour Grove
   c. Hanger Hill Wood
   d. Clipstone Junction

8. Villa Real is a neighbourhood (a *barrio)* on the west edge of Buenos Aires

Key Answer
* Queen Oak

MAP
15

1. 8 (from north to south: Park Lodge, Park Side, Hare Park, Park Gate Farm, Chatsworth Park [Deer Park], Park Wood, Old Park Plantation)

2. A plantation

3. The word 'End'

4. 3

5. Jumble Coppice

6. The Peak District

7. Mary Queen of Scots (from Jubilee Rock, travel south down the contour line that passes through its 'K' till you reach the first 'H' in The Hunting Tower. Travel west till you reach the 'Deer' below Chatsworth Park, and south until you reach the possibly dubious Queen Mary's Bower)

8. An area of non-coniferous trees on access land, just a little to the left of the very top right corner, at 275m

Key Answer

* 5

MAP
16

1. Sun Down

2. 2 (1 west of Glade Farm, 1 north-east of Glade Farm)

3. The Springhill Farm

4. Kent (it runs from Canterbury through to Wroxeter)

5. The A5190, which crosses a 165m contour line by its western edge as it goes through Gorsty Ley

6. 22 (A5190 ÷ A5 = 1038 ÷ M6 = 173 − 151m point west of Barracks Lane = 22)

7. 2009 (it is known as the Staffordshire Hoard, and was found a short distance south-west of Hammerwich)

8. a. Watling Street
   b. Lichfield Road
   c. Whitacre Lane
   d. Burntwood Green

🔍 **Key Answer**
   * Burntwood Green (north of Apple Tree Farm)

MAP
17

1. Westminster Farm

2. A recreation, leisure or sports centre

3. 100m (45m at east edge of map, to 145m above the 'o' of Lloyd's)

4. Broseley

5. B4373 (Cockshot Mound, to Ladywood, to A4169, then left north of Lightmoor Junction, and right along second contour to B4373 north of roundabout)

6. The Iron Bridge

7. a. Stocking Mound
   b. The Deerleap
   c. Captain's Coppice
   d. Lodge Lane

8. A rabbit burrow

Key Answer

* Lodge Lane

MAP

18

1. 3 (Royal Shakespeare Theatre, Shakespeare's Avon Way and Shakespeare's Way)

2. 75m

3. Coachroad Covert

4. To the south-west of the map, south of the B439 and north of the cemetery

5. Welcombe Hills Country Park (A4390 + B4632 = 9022 = 90 + 22 = 112, to 111m peak, just west of the Welcombe Hills Country Park symbol)

6. Elizabeth, Lady Barnard (nee Hall, formely Nash), Shakespeare's granddaughter, died in 1670. (1+6+7+0 = 14)

7. a. Bluecap Covert
   b. Rosebird Centre
   c. The Belt
   d. Clifford Lane
   e. Bishopton
   f. Potato Hill

8. Mark Phillips, a nineteenth-century MP who commissioned Welcombe as a stately home (it is now a hotel)

Key Answer

* Monarch's Way

MAP
19

1. Shakespeare's Way

2. 118m

3. A mast (248m air survey point west of Baker's Hill, to mast south of South Hill Farm)

4. A public house, between Northdown Farm and South Hill Farm

5. The circle is said to be uncountable (current estimates say 77 stones, but a few fragments are small enough to permit debate as to whether they are separate or part of another stone). The clue relates to the idea that if the stones are uncountable then a pedant might claim it should be 'less' not 'fewer' stones

6. Northdown, Railway, Turnpikehill and Windmill

7. 200m (Springhill Farm, Hirons Hill Farm, Windmill Farm and Brighthill Farm)

8. It is not possible without mechanical assistance (according to long-established local legend recorded by William Camden in 1610, a king was passing the ridge when a witch, named Mother Shipton, challenged him to take seven steps from where he was, and if he could still see Long Compton village, he would be sure to become King of all England. He took his steps, but the witch caused the hill to rise in front of him, blocking the view. Because he'd failed, she turned him into the King Stone, his army into the King's Men circle and some traitorous knights planning against him into the Whispering Knights cairn. Finally, she transformed herself into a hawthorn bush at the King Stone's feet, to guard her work)

⌕ **Key Answer**
 * Brighthill Farm

MAP
20

1. 7 (Carreg Gerwynau, Carreg Lwyd, Carreg Onnen Bay, Carreg Gybi, Carreg y Wrach, Carreg Ddu and Carreg Onnen)

2. Pembrokeshire

3. 14 (1 east of Ynys Onnen, 3 east of Llanwnwr, 2 north-west and 1 south-east of Carreg Lwyd, 1 west of Tre-fisheg, 1 near the coast to the far west of Rhos Howell, 1 west of North Pole, 1 south-west of Llandruidion and 2 south and 1 south-east of Trefasser Cross)

4. The area is known for observing porpoises, seals, other marine mammals and migrating birds heading south for winter

5. Island

6. Pool

7. a. Llan*druid*ion

    b. Harmony

    c. Lady's Gate

    d. North Pole

8. Ynys Onnen (Phone at Castell-boeth to Treathro. Contour is 75, 76m point is to the west, near a spring. The land rises to the south, blocking the view in that direction)

🔍 **Key Answer**

* Ynys

MAP

21

1. 4 (Boston Lodge Halt, Tygwyn Station and 2 stations near the Business Park which appear unnamed on the map, but are actually both called Minffordd Station and are two adjacent stations operated entirely separately from each other)

2. 81m, north-west of Castelldeudraeth

3. Boston Lodge Halt

4. Ynys Llanfihangel-y-traethau

5. Dangerous tides

6. Italy

7. Parking, near Abergafren (south of Ynys, follow A-road to Glan-y-wern, to rail bridge, to Well at Draenogan, to Well at Llechollwyn, to yellow road to Parking)

8. 1080 (27 + 36 + 2 + 2 + 44 + 4 + 81 + 50 + 10 + 30 + 20 + 3 + 10 + 33 + 44 + 10 + 20 + 69 + 30 + 58 + 497)

Key Answer

* Castle

MAP
22

1. A recreation, leisure or sports centre, bicycle hire and indoor rock climbing

2. Morfa Common

3. The Police Station

4. 3 (Alice, Helen and Victoria)

5. Anglesey, or Ynys Môn in Welsh

6. Pont Peblig (Tyddyn-Alice Farm, Ty'rallt Farm, Pant Farm, 23)

7. Hendy Covert ('Handy Covert')

8. Back where you started (Tal-y-foel Pier to a spring near Aber Bridge, to the hill marked 48m, to the A487 and then west to Tal-y-foel Pier)

Key Answer

* Bridge

MAP

23

1. Deganwy Castle

2. A55

3. 15 (1 between Deganwy and Tywyn, 6 in Tywyn, 5 in Conwy, 3 in Gyffin)

4. Conwy Castle

5. The Clubhouse

6. The Tubular Bridge (after *Tubular Bells*)

7. 38 (path leads east to Bryn-seiri Road. Nearest chevron to the east. Tree is shortly before coastline. The 'n' is in Tywyn. Black ground survey height '38' is to the north of that)

8. The smallest house in Great Britain

Key Answer

* 1133 (547 x 2 = 1094 + 39)

MAP
24

1. Cemeteries (2 cemeteries: 1 east of the B1049 and 1 east of Parker's Piece. 1 farm: River Farm)

2. 4 (1 in the second column, 1 between the second and third columns and 2 in the third column)

3. 13m (from the cycle hire in the centre of Cambridge, south-west to cycle hire near Newnham Croft and on to 13m mark on Grantchester Road)

4. 16 (counting the two semi-detached houses as separate)

5. Clare (Br.), Jesus (Close) and Newnham (Croft)

6. Peterhouse, founded in 1284

7. Football, at Parker's Piece (the University of Cambridge Football Club Laws, first used on the common, were adopted by the Football Association in 1863)

8. Punting (it is the only one of the five that is written on the map in blue)

Key Answer

* Fen Rivers Way

MAP
25

1. Suffolk

2. 3 (1 in Horning, 1 near the Horning Ferry Drainage Mill and 1 at Ranworth)

3. Horning Marshes (within the heavily coloured 25m contour line, the third 5m contour above the 10m line as shown at Upper Street)

4. South of Brown's Hill

5. Each appears as part of the name of a broad (Burnt*fen* Broad, Malt*house* Broad, Cock*shoot* Broad and Ran*worth* Broad)

6. They are medieval peat quarries that flooded as sea levels rose over the centuries

7. *Tit*he Barn, *Swan* Hotel, *Cock*shoot Dike, *Cock*shoot Broad, *Owl*'s Grove; *Boa*t Yard, *Horse* Marsh, B*ram*blehill, Pondhead Pl*ant*ation, *Pit* Road, The Bo*xes*

8. Three non-coniferous tree symbols, a short distance to the west of the Swan Hotel in Horning

> ### Key Answer
> * Marina

MAP
26

1. Bramble Hill

2. 3 (Melton Hall, Haddon Hall and Methersgate Hall)

3. 5 (1 east of Melton Hall, 1 below the second 'D' of Woodbridge, 1 west of Mill Hills, 1 between the two 'B1079' legends and 1 north of the blue museum symbol)

4. Deben Wood (from the River Deben)

5. They all appear within the names of farms (Ferry Farm, Witchpit Farm, Trott's Farm and Sutton Hoo Farm)

6. Suffolk

7. Potash Farm ($1152 - 1083 = 69 + 6 = 75 \div 3 = 25$)

8. Mrs Edith Pretty (after giving the trove to the British Museum, she was offered a CBE in recognition of the largest ever donation to the British nation made by a living person – she declined)

Key Answer

* Railway track

MAP
27

1. 4 (Ampthill Park House, Houghton House, Kingsdown House and Fordfield House)

2. There are 4 more farms than wells (9 farms: Lower Farm, Lodge Piece Farm, Park Farm, Ossory Farm, Warren Farm, Littlepark Farm, Fordfield Farm, Grange Stud Farm and Kiln Farm. 5 wells: 1 southeast of the Engineering Research Establishment, 2 at Lower Farm, 1 at Millbrook church and 1 at Fordfield Farm)

3. 7 (125 aerial near Ampthill Park, 118 ground near Gravelpit Plantation)

4. Postern Piece

5. Lancelot

6. a. In*dust*rial Estate
   b. *Grave*lpit Plantation
   c. Engineering Re*search* Establishment
   d. Re*servo*ir
   e. Po*stern* Piece

7. Redbourne School and College (75m line near south of map, to east edge near centre of map, south of a footpath. Then south-south-west to a triangular lake, then west to 77 below Littlepark Farm. Other 77m point is to south-east by name of Grange Stud Farm. Redbourne's buildings are closer)

8. King Henry VIII and Queen Catherine of Aragon

◯ **Key Answer**

* Park

MAP
28

1. Grand Union Canal

2. Redmoor

3. The Enigma Machine

4. 5 (2 train stations, 1 bus/coach station, 1 fire station, 1 police station)

5. 200 (5 × 4146 ÷ 100 = 207.3)

6. d. Weir is the only one that appears on the map as a separate word

7. a. Blue Lagoon Park
   b. Towing Path
   c. Fenny Stratford
   d. Water Eaton

8. Alan Mathison Turing (the letters are reversed and spaces removed, and then the block of text is broken up by spaces)

Key Answer
* Water Eaton

1. 3 (Eton, Windsor and Old Windsor)

2. Queen Anne (Queen Anne's Gate)

3. 8 (B3026, B376, B3022, M4, B470, B3021, A322 and A308)

4. Peter's Hill

5. Henry I, although it was built by William the Conqueror

6. Frogmore House (The Gallop and The Long Walk, past Hog Common to Frogmore)

7. Herne the Hunter (According to *The Merry Wives of Windsor* by William Shakespeare, this is the ghost of a former Windsor forester who haunts a particular oak tree at midnight in winter. This might possibly refer to a hunter named Richard Horne who was caught poaching during King Henry VIII's reign)

8. a. Moram Lodge
   b. Royal Mausoleum
   c. The Brocas
   d. Tileplace Farm

Key Answer

* The Gallop

MAP
30

1. The Derby

2. Nohome Farm

3. 10 (Stables x 4, Buckle, Grand Stand, Paddock, Race Course x 2, Stud Farm)

4. Golf

5. Chalk Lane and The Paddock (the line goes through Ashley Road, Langley Vale Road, Langley Vale and Langley Vale Farm)

6. Hats (with fascinators, typically)

7. a. Ebbisham Lane
   b. Ashley Road
   c. Wingfield Stud Farm
   d. Tattenham Corner

8. 34 (the initial buildings are at 165m, Nohome Farm is at 100m, and there are two telephones and three railway stations. 65 × 5 = 325. B291 is the B-road with the largest number, so 325 − 291 = 34)

> **Key Answer**
> * Viewpoint

MAP
31

1. The Greenwich (or Prime) Meridian, marking the internationally agreed line of zero longitude (in fact, the current modern standard, the IERS Reference Meridian, is calculated precisely by reference to the Earth's mass, and passes a little over 100m away from the Greenwich Meridian)

2. The 3rd (with 5 stations)

3. 10 (A102, A200, A206, A1206, A2209, A2210, A2211, B210, B212 and B220)

4. Just one, inside a lake in Greenwich Park (the Isle of Dogs is a peninsula)

5. A (tea) clipper (clippers were three-masted ships designed for speed over cargo space)

6. Police HQ, towards the south end of the A2211 on the map

7. Blackwall, Hollyhedge, Maritime and Observatory

8. Anne of Denmark, wife of James I (The Queen's House)

Key Answer
* A2

MAP

32

1. Cherrytree Hole south of Famine Down

2. 10 (1 next to the A2 roundabout, 4 south of Bere Farm, 1 south of those, 2 east of Broadlees, 2 on the cliff between Fox Hill Down and Langdon Hole)

3. Chalk

4. d. SHIP (the others all appear on the map as part of a place name)

5. 8 (Bowesfield Farm Boarding Kennels, Brickfield Cottages, Bere Wood, Bere Farm, Broadlees, Broadlees Bottom, Bleriot Memorial and The Camber)

6. Wallett's Court (A158 + A20 + A2 = 180 − 125 [at Duke of York's Royal Military School] = 55 + 20 [2 × 10 letters in Famine Down] = 75m line passing through words 'Wallett's Court (Hotel)')

7. Around 35 hours (the Channel is approximately 21 miles at its narrowest point)

8. Broadlees, Brickfield, Cherrytree, Military

Key Answer
* Bere Wood

MAP
33

1. Greenwood

2. Peculiar's Farm

3. Cotchford, Kilnwood, Shawhurst, Standing

4. 17 (Jack's Farm, Cotchford Farm, Kilnwood Farm, Posingford Farm, Ryecroft Farm, Fincham Farm, Tile Barn Farm, Neaves Farm, Hart's Farm, Shawhurst Farm, Podlea Flock Farm, Peculiar's Farm, Spring Farm, New Lodge Farm, Cobbers Farm, Kidd's Hill Farm and Deerswood Farm)

5. 170 (Pillow Mound is directly north of the aerial survey height number just above Ashdown Forest)

6. 500 acres (Five Hundred Acre Wood)

7. a. Lone Oak Hall
   b. Black Hill
   c. Jumper's Town
   d. Wren's Warren
   e. Cabbagestalk

8. 27 (Gils Lap to B2026 to junction with road to Kidd's Hill, and along to ford)

> **Key Answer**
> * King's Standing

MAP
34

1. 16 acres

2. 3 (1 to the right of Bough Beech, 1 to the right of Hever and 1 to the left of Meechlands Farm)

3. Pigdown and Dogpits

4. Elmsbridge, Greenland, Newhouse and Polebrook

5. Wilderness Farm, west of Avebury Down

6. Anne Boleyn

7. Gravelpits (Air Shaft in Markbeech Wood, to Greenland Farm, to The Red House, to Lockskinners Farm, and north)

8. A wooded hill/elevated area

Key Answer

* Wychwood Fruit Farm

MAP

35

1. 191m

2. Pan Bridge

3. Place of worship, post office, public telephone, public house – and, if you consider it an amenity, a milestone

4. It is man-made (at almost 130ft, it is the tallest prehistoric man-made hill in Europe)

5. Manor Farm, west of Avebury Down

6. Rutlands Farm

7. 169 (Tumuli or Tumulus appear 17 times, and the lowest height next to a car park is 152, to the west of Silbury Hill)

8. Avebury Manor (start at the mound south of West Kennet Long Barrow, to 183m mark, to 187m on Silbury Hill, to tumuli south of Avebury Down, and west to Avebury Manor)

Key Answer

* Park

MAP
36

1. Scotland

2. Lions

3. The Grove

4. 10 (Rush Pool, Dod Pool, Tomkins Pool, Half Mile Pond, Ford Pond, Petit Jean's Island Pond, Great Island Pond, Little Island Pond, Upper Pond, Mill Pond)

5. a. Dairy Coppice
   b. Heaven's Gate
   c. Icehouse Piece
   d. Long Hedgerow

6. Open itself to the public on a commercial basis

7. Carpenter, Hitcombe, Longhedge, Newbury, Ragland, Rushpool and Woodhouse

8. Horningsham Common Plantation (Between the peak of Park Hill and the Safari Park, add and average $200 + 185 + 175 + 165 + 155 = 880 \div 5 = 176$. Divide this by 8 [Dertford's Wood, High Wood, Ragland Coppice, Green's Coppice, Hazel Coppice, Cowern Coppice, Nockatt Coppice, Dairy Coppice] $= 22 \times 10 = 220$, to be found near the centre of the bottom left grid square, and north to answer)

🔍 **Key Answer**

* Heaven's Gate

MAP
37

1. The remains of St Michael's Church (the tower still stands as a local landmark)

2. King Arthur

3. Rhyne (Great Withy Rhyne, Read Mead Rhyne, Actis Mead Rhyne and Old Rhyne. In the dialect of the South-West of England, the word *rhyne* means a large open ditch or drain)

4. Wearyall Hill and Cow Bridge

5. A post office (3 × 4 = 12. 12m height just north of Museum symbol south of town. North to A361, left at T-junction, and again on white road north of Abbey, and right past church to orange road)

6. Avalon (Ynyr yr Afalon, 'The Isle of Avalon')

7. a. Rifle Range
   b. Read Mead Rhyne
   c. Black Pit Drove
   d. Tin Bridge Farm

8. He was hung, drawn and quartered (Richard Whiting was executed in 1539 by King Henry VIII for treason, due to his refusal to renounce the Pope)

Key Answer
* 352 (361 − 9)

MAP

38

1. Giant's Head Farmhouse

2. 8 (Wancombe Bottom, Yelcombe Bottom, Park Mead Bottom, Oxencombe Bottom, Francombe Bottom, Higher Hill Bottom, Bramble Bottom and Pound Bottom)

3. 12 (1 on Giant Hill, 1 near Oxencombe Bottom, 2 on Dickley Hill, 7 along the path on Green Hill and 1 on Smacam Down)

4. 'Rude'

5. b. Bow's – Bow's Hill is the only one of the four that does not have a good view of The Giant (line of sight is obscured by Black Hill, which is both higher and more westerly)

6. Portland Bill

7. 4 November 1694

8. Foxhills (247m near Giant's Head Farmhouse to path west and south to Settlement, south again to edge of Black Hill, to Hail Wood, to Foxhills)

🔍 Key Answer

* Dickley Hill

MAP
39

1. 3 (1 riverside south of Southpark Wood, 1 next to the road south of Humphrey's Cross and 1 east of Holy Brook)

2. Halfmoon

3. Woods (Southpark Wood and North Wood)

4. Dartmoor (which Buckfastleigh is on the edge of)

5. Blackmoor, Glebelands, Hannaford and Camphill

6. a. Merryfield
   b. Humphrey's Cross
   c. Button
   d. Holy Brook

7. Dirty Dick (Squire Richard Cabell, who lived in Brook Hall)

8. Hapstead Camphill (201 + 178 = 379 + 1 = 380 ÷ 10 = 38 + 110 + 150 + 180 + 210 + 240 + 260 = 1188 + 2 = 1190 ÷ 10 = 119 rearranged to 191)

Key Answer
* King

MAP

40

1. 7 (1 unnamed 'caves' location at Barras Nose, 1 at Tintagel Head, 1 at Glebe Cliff, 1 at Dennis Scale, 1 at Hole Beach, 2 at Port William)

2. The Sisters

3. His mother, Igraine

4. Downrow

5. Glebe Cliff ('Grebe')

6. They appear on the map within words starting with 'Tre'

7. Dennis Scale (Trevillick Farm to T-junction north of Trewarmett, to coast north of Vean Hole, to Dennis Point)

8. Cornishmen (according to the Cornish antiquary Richard Carew in 1602)

NOTES

NOTES

ORDNANCE SURVEY MAP INFORMATION

The Ordnance Survey Great British Treasure Hunt features our celebrated OS Explorer mapping, enlarged slightly from the familiar scale of 1:25 000 to 1:20 000 to improve the puzzle experience. The iconic OS Explorer map is used daily by thousands of people, from ramblers to rock climbers. The first time maps were produced at the 1:25 000 scale (2½ inches on the map being equivalent to 1 mile on the ground, or 4cm to 1km) was in the early twentieth century, but back then only the military had access to this level of detail on a paper map; the first military map from Ordnance Survey covered East Anglia.

Mapping was extremely important during the two world wars, but it wasn't until 1938 that it was suggested that a series of maps be produced for the general public. The thinking was that if this idea took off in schools, then the mapping might eventually cover the whole of Great Britain to give outdoors enthusiasts unrivalled access to the countryside. The first experimental (or Provisional) maps at this scale appeared after the Second World War ended in 1945.

Interest in leisure time spent in the countryside began to grow, and more consideration was given to 1:25 000 mapping. In 1972 the first Outdoor Leisure (OL) map was published, of the Dark Peak area of the Peak District, and subsequently other OL maps were published, concentrating on the national parks and areas of outstanding natural beauty. As a result of the success of the Outdoor Leisure maps, many other maps were redesigned. These were called Pathfinders, and they covered England and Wales, showing all public rights of way and making it easier to plan walking routes.

The first OS Explorer maps were published in 1994, replacing the popular Pathfinder series and making our maps even more user-friendly. On average the OS Explorer maps covered three times the area of the Pathfinders and were six times bigger than the original Outdoor Leisure maps at this scale. The additional tourist and leisure information – including viewpoints, pubs, picnic sites – resulted in an amazing level of detail.

By 2003, every Pathfinder and Outdoor Leisure map had been converted to the OS Explorer series and in 2004, following the Countryside and Rights of Way Act 2000, areas of open access were depicted. These days, if you buy an OS Explorer map you also get a free mobile download to use in our award-winning OS Maps app.

Not sure which leisure map you need for your next adventure? Here's a handy comparison:

OS Explorer 1:25 000 (4cm to 1km or 2½ inches to the mile)

OS Explorer is the nation's most popular leisure map. It features footpaths, rights of way and open access land, and is recommended for walking, running and horse riding. The OS Explorer map covers a smaller area than the OS Landranger map, but presents the landscape in more detail, aiding navigation and making it the perfect accompaniment on an adventure. It also highlights tourist information and points of interest, including viewpoints and pubs.

OS Landranger 1:50 000 (2cm to 1km or 1¼ inches to the mile)

OS Landranger aids the planning of the perfect short break in Great Britain and is a vital resource for identifying opportunities in both towns and countryside. It displays larger areas of the country than OS Explorer, making it more suitable for touring an area by car or by bicycle, helping you access the best an area has to offer.

OS Road 1:250 000 (1cm to 2.5km or 1 inch to 4 miles)

Ideal for navigating and planning any road journey, the OS Road series helps you get to your destination. The range covers the whole of Great Britain and shows all motorways, primary routes and A-roads, plus detailed tourist information including National Parks, World Heritage Sites and a useful town and city gazetteer.

OS SHEET INDEX

	Puzzle map and feature	County/Council area	OS map sheet			Centre point	1 km reference
1	Callanish, Isle of Lewis	Na h-Eileanan Siar (Western Isles)	459	13	2	NB 21151 33131	NB 21 33
2	Skye Bridge	Highland	412	33	2	NG 74612 27106	NG 74 27
3	Loch Ness	Highland	416	24	1	NH 49586 29545	NH 49 29
4	Ben Nevis	Highland	392	41	1	NN 16660 71284	NN 16 71
5	Inveraray	Argyll and Bute	OL37	56	2	NN 09534 08500	NN 09 08
6	Kelvingrove, Glasgow	Glasgow City	342	64	3	NS 56777 66265	NS 56 66
7	The Forth Bridges	Edinburgh/Fife	350	65	3	NT 12523 79604	NT 12 79
8	Lindisfarne	Northumberland	340	75	3	NU 13028 42334	NU 13 42
9	Housesteads, Hadrian's Wall	Northumberland	OL43	87	3	NY 78903 68913	NY 78 68
10	St Bees Head	Cumbria	303	89	4	NX 95275 13518	NX 95 13
11	Wray Castle, Lake Windermere	Cumbria	OL7	90	4	NY 37611 01071	NY 37 01
12	Whitby Abbey	North Yorkshire	OL27	94	4	NZ 90422 11194	NZ 90 11
13	Humber Bridge	East Riding of Yorkshire/ Lincolnshire	281	107	4	TA 02394 25304	TA 02 25
14	Sherwood Forest	Nottinghamshire	270	120	4	SK 61960 67908	SK 61 67
15	Chatsworth House	Derbyshire	OL24	119	4	SK 25592 70153	SK 25 70
16	Hammerwich	Staffordshire	244	139	6	SK 06995 07550	SK 06 07
17	Ironbridge	Shropshire	242	127	6	SJ 67618 03454	SJ 67 03
18	Stratford-upon-Avon	Warwickshire	205	151	5	SP 20170 54978	SP 20 54
19	Rollright Stones	Oxfordshire/Warwickshire	191	151	8	SP 29663 31068	SP 29 31
20	Strumble Head	Pembrokeshire	OL35	157	6	SM 89868 39379	SM 89 39
21	Portmeirion	Gwynedd	OL18	124	6	SH 59021 37177	SH 59 37
22	Caernarfon Castle	Gwynedd	OL17	115	6	SH 47792 62616	SH 47 62
23	Conwy Suspension Bridge	Clwyd	OL17	115	6	SH 78441 77520	SH 78 77
24	Cambridge	Cambridgeshire	209	154	5	TL 44757 58637	TL 44 58
25	The Broads	Norfolk	OL40	134	5	TG 35513 17221	TG 35 17
26	Sutton Hoo	Suffolk	197	169	5	TM 28846 49077	TM 28 49
27	Ampthill	Bedfordshire	193	153	5	TL 02709 38579	TL 02 38
28	Bletchley Park	Buckinghamshire	192	152	5	SP 86391 33951	SP 86 33
29	Windsor Castle	Berkshire	160	175	8	SU 97131 76995	SU 97 76
30	Epsom Race Course	Surrey	146	187	8	TQ 21759 58580	TQ 21 58
31	Greenwich	Greater London	161	177	8	TQ 38873 77323	TQ 38 77
32	White Cliffs of Dover	Kent	138	179	8	TR 33906 43679	TR 33 43
33	Ashdown Forest	East Sussex	135	188	8	TQ 46888 33891	TQ 46 33
34	Hever Castle	Kent	147	188	8	TQ 47787 45270	TQ 47 45
35	Avebury	Wiltshire	157	173	8	SU 10168 69938	SU 10 69
36	Longleat	Wiltshire	143	183	7	ST 80898 43018	ST 80 43
37	Glastonbury Tor	Somerset	141	183	7	ST 51168 38599	ST 51 38
38	Cerne Abbas	Dorset	117	194	7	ST 66643 01672	ST 66 01
39	Buckfastleigh	Devon	OL28	202	7	SX 71299 67689	SX 71 67
40	Tintagel Castle	Cornwall	111	200	7	SX 05816 88616	SX 05 88

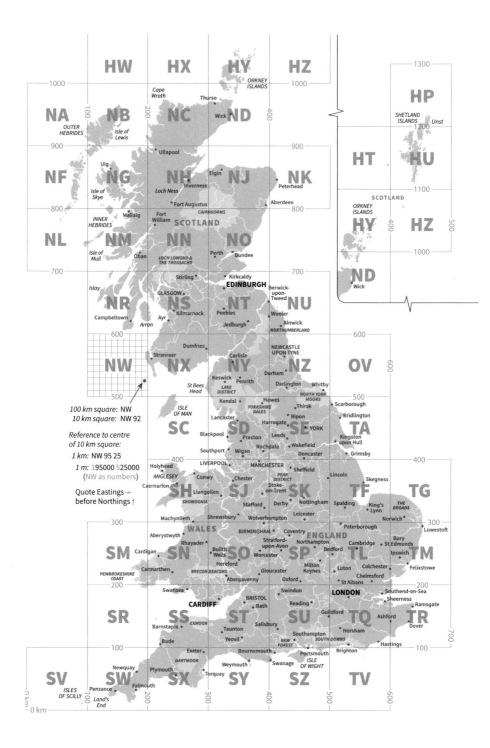

HW HX HY HZ

1300

HP

SHETLAND ISLANDS Unst

1200

HT HU

SCOTLAND

ORKNEY ISLANDS

HY HZ

500

1100

1000

ND

Wick

ORKNEY ISLANDS

Cape Wrath   Thurso

1000

NA NB NC ND

OUTER HEBRIDES   Isle of Lewis   Wick

100   200   400

900

900

Ullapool

NF NG NH NJ NK

Uig   Elgin   Peterhead
Isle of Skye   Inverness
Loch Ness   Fort Augustus

800

800

CAIRNGORMS

Aberdeen

NL NM NN NO

INNER HEBRIDES   Mallaig   Fort William   SCOTLAND
Isle of Mull   Oban   LOCH LOMOND & THE TROSSACHS   Perth   Dundee

700

700

Islay   Stirling   Kirkcaldy
GLASGOW   EDINBURGH   Berwick-upon-Tweed

NR NS NT NU

Campbeltown   Ayr   Kilmarnock   Peebles   Wooler
Arran   Jedburgh   Alnwick   NORTHUMBERLAND

600

Dumfries   NEWCASTLE UPON TYNE   600

NW NX NY NZ OV

Stranraer   Carlisle
Keswick   Penrith   Durham   Whitby
Darlington

500   St Bees Head   LAKE DISTRICT   NORTH YORK MOORS   500

100 km square: NW   ISLE OF MAN   Kendal   Hawes   Thirsk   Scarborough
10 km square: NW 92   YORKSHIRE DALES   Ripon   Bridlington

Reference to centre of 10 km square: SC   SD   SE   TA

1 km: NW 95 25   Lancaster   Harrogate   YORK   Kingston upon Hull
1 m: 195000 525000   Blackpool   Preston   Leeds   Grimsby
(NW as numbers)   Southport   Rochdale   Wakefield
Wigan   Doncaster

Quote Eastings →   400   LIVERPOOL   MANCHESTER   Sheffield   400
before Northings ↑   Holyhead   Chester   Lincoln   Skegness
ANGLESEY   Conwy   Stoke-on-Trent   PEAK DISTRICT
Caernarfon   SH   SJ   SK   TF   TG

Llangollen   Derby   Nottingham   Spalding   THE BROADS
SNOWDONIA   Stafford   Leicester   King's Lynn   Norwich
Machynlleth   Shrewsbury   Wolverhampton   Peterborough   Lowestoft

300   WALES   BIRMINGHAM   Coventry   ENGLAND   300
Aberystwyth   Rhayader   Stratford-upon-Avon   Northampton   Cambridge   Bury St Edmunds
SM   SN   Builth Wells   SO   Worcester   SP   Bedford   TL   Ipswich   TM
Cardigan   Hereford   Milton Keynes   Luton   Colchester   Felixstowe
PEMBROKESHIRE COAST   Carmarthen   BRECON BEACONS   Gloucester   Oxford   Chelmsford
200   Abergavenny   St Albans   200
Swansea   BRISTOL   Swindon   LONDON   Southend-on-Sea
CARDIFF   Bath   Reading   Sheerness
SR   SS   ST   Guildford   SU   TQ   Ramsgate
Barnstaple   EXMOOR   Taunton   Salisbury   Horsham   TR   Dover
Bude   Yeovil   Southampton   SOUTH DOWNS   Ashford
100   NEW FOREST   Bournemouth   Portsmouth   Brighton   Hastings   100
Exeter   DARTMOOR   Weymouth   Swanage   ISLE OF WIGHT
SV   Newquay   Plymouth   SX   SY   SZ   TV
ISLES OF SCILLY   Penzance   Torquay
SW   Falmouth
Land's End

0 km   100   200   300   400   500   600   700

0 km

CREDITS

Trapeze would like to thank everyone at Orion who worked on the publication of *The Ordnance Survey Great British Treasure Hunt* in the UK.

Editorial: Jamie Coleman, Georgia Goodall, Sarah Fortune, Jane Hughes. Copy editor: Abi Waters. Proofreader: Lorraine Jerram. Contracts: Anne Goddard, Paul Bulos. Design: Rabab Adams, Lucie Stericker, Helen Ewing, Julyan Bayes. Finance: Jennifer Muchan, Elizabeth Beaumont, Ibukun Ademefun, Jasdip Nandra, Rabale Mustafa, Afeera Ahmed. Marketing: Helena Fouracre. Production: Claire Keep, Fiona McIntosh. Publicity: Alainna Hadjigeorgiou. Sales: Jen Wilson, Esther Waters, Rachael Hum, Ellie Kyrke-Smith, Viki Cheung, Dominic Smith, Barbara Ronan, Maggy Park. Rights: Susan Howe, Richard King, Krystyna Kujawinksa, Jessue Purdue. Operations: Jo Jacobs, Sharon Willis, Lisa Pryde.

ACKNOWLEDGEMENTS

Thank you to the many people who have worked
hard to make this book happen, including:

Nick Giles, Paul McGonigal, Mark Wolstenholme, Carolyne Lawton, Daphne Berghorst, Gemma Bell, Liz Beverley, Gemma Jones, Mandy Brereton, Alex Jacob, Jo Lines, Jim Goldsmith, Keegan Wilson, Sam Lovell, David Jones, Emily Bennett, the OS Consumer Team, the OS Cartographic Production Team, Julia Bradbury, Adam Gauntlett, Orion Publishing and Tim Dedopulos.

Ordnance Survey

Fancy brushing up on your map reading skills and solving even more fiendish puzzles? Why not get yourself copies of *The Ordnance Survey Puzzle Book* and *The Ordnance Survey Puzzle Tour of Britain*, and pit your wits against Britain's greatest map makers?

Share your adventures and puzzle-solving with us:

os.uk/blog

@ordnancesurvey

@OSLeisure

@osmapping

Help us make the next generation of readers

We – both author and publisher – hope you enjoyed this book. We believe that you can become a reader at any time in your life, but we'd love your help to give the next generation a head start.

Did you know that 9 per cent of children don't have a book of their own in their home, rising to 13 per cent in disadvantaged families*? We'd like to try to change that by asking you to consider the role you could play in helping to build readers of the future.

We'd love you to think of sharing, borrowing, reading, buying or talking about a book with a child in your life and spreading the love of reading. We want to make sure the next generation continue to have access to books, wherever they come from.

And if you would like to consider donating to charities that help fund literacy projects, find out more at **www.literacytrust.org.uk** and **www.booktrust.org.uk**.

THANK YOU

*As reported by the National Literacy Trust

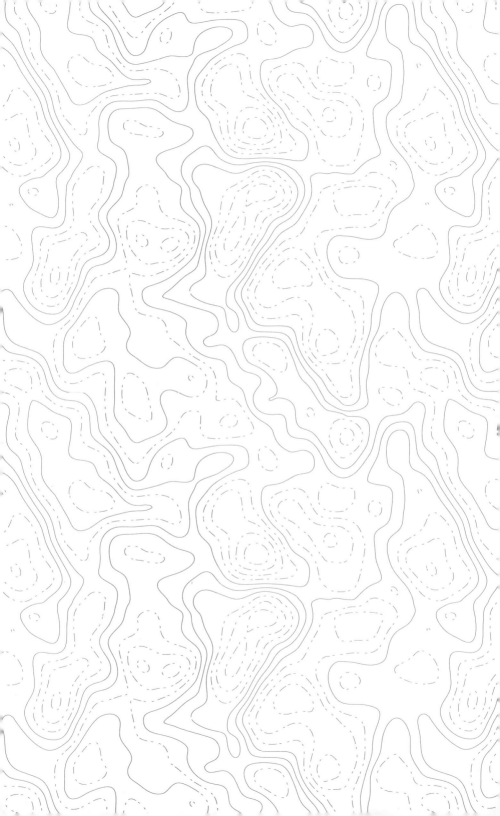